KETO DIET FOR BEGINNERS

© Copyright 2018 - All rights reserved.

The contents of this book may not be reproduced, duplicated or transmitted without direct written permission from the author.

Under no circumstances will any legal responsibility or blame be held against the publisher for any reparation, damages, or monetary loss due to the information herein, either directly or indirectly.

Legal Notice:

This book is copyright protected. This is only for personal use. You cannot amend, distribute, sell, use, quote or paraphrase any part or the content within this book without the consent of the author.

Disclaimer Notice:

Please note the information contained within this document is for educational and entertainment purposes only. Every attempt has been made to provide accurate, up to date and reliable complete information. No warranties of any kind are expressed or implied. Readers acknowledge that the author is not engaging in the rendering of legal, financial, medical or professional advice. The content of this book has been derived from various sources. Please consult a licensed professional before attempting any techniques outlined in this book.

By reading this document, the reader agrees that under no circumstances is the author responsible for any losses, direct or indirect, which are incurred as a result of the use of information contained within this document, including, but not limited to, — errors, omissions, or inaccuracies.

DEDICATION

We thank our many friends and family members for their support and helpful suggestions: Kate, Rosy, Very, Simo, Rita, Angy, Marika, Gerry, Cynthia, Flo, Roby and Alex.

We give thanks to God for the incredible energy, clarity, and support we received in bringing forth this book.

Table of Contents

Introduction 1
Chapter One: Overview of Ketogenic Diet 3
   Ketogenic diet and its history 4
      Introduction of the low-carb diet 4
      The fall of the Ketogenic Diet 5
      Comeback of the Low-carb diets 6
Macronutrients and Micronutrients 8
      Carbohydrates 9
      Proteins 9
      Fats 10
   Micronutrients in a Keto diet 12
Chapter Two: What Exactly is a Ketogenic Diet? 14
   What is Ketosis and how does it work? 14
   What are Ketones? 16
   Types of Ketogenic Diets 19
      Standard Ketogenic Diet (SKD) 19
      Cyclical Ketogenic diet (CKD) 19
      Targeted Ketogenic diet (TKD) 19
      High-protein Ketogenic diet 20
   Is Ketogenic diet for everyone? 20
   Side-effects of the Ketogenic diet 21
   How can you enter ketosis effectively? 22

Chapter Three: What to Eat and What not to Eat 24

What to eat? 24

- Vegetables that grow above the ground 24
- Other Vegetables 25
- Healthy Fats 26
- Fruit 27
- Meatless Proteins 27
- Condiments 28
- Meat 28
- Seafood and Fish 29
- Eggs 29
- High-fat Sauces, Natural Fat 30
- Drinks that are allowed 32

What not to eat? 33

- Sugar 33
- Starch 34
- Beer 35
- Fruit 35
- Margarine 35
- Tubers and Root vegetables 35
- Processed food 36

Other Keto-approved food that you can hog on 36

Grocery Shopping Lists 37

- Proteins 37

Staples needed in your kitchen 38

Oils and Spices 38

Foods rich in Omega-3 fatty acids 39

Dairy products 39

Keto-friendly sweeteners (one or two of them) 39

Vegetables 40

Fruit 41

Chapter Four: Food Sensitivity 42

How will I know if I have food intolerance? 43

Going dairy-free 45

Dairy-free food that you can consume 48

Chapter Five: Tips and Guidelines 50

Common mistakes to avoid 50

Don't be scared of fat 50

Water is important 51

Get Salty 51

Dairy is good but don't go overboard 52

Know your WHY factor 52

Too much protein isn't good 53

Stop snacking often 53

No more habit-eating 54

Sleep is essential 54

Stress management 54

Don't eat the same meal every time 55

No cheat days 55

Quick tips you can follow 55

Chapter Six: Frequently Asked Questions (FAQs) 58

Chapter Seven: Lose 20 pounds in 30 days 64

Following the rules 64

Structured 30-day meal plan 67

Shopping Lists 72

    Dairy and Eggs 72

    Meat and Fish 73

    Vegetables and Fruit 74

    Herbs and Spices 75

    Oils and Condiments 77

    Baking goods & non-dairy products 77

    Nuts and Seeds 78

    Others 79

Chapter Eight: Smoothies and Smoothie-bowl Recipes 80

Strawberry Shake 80

Pumpkin Chai Smoothie 82

Spinach Avocado Green Smoothie 83

Avocado Smoothie 84

Blueberry Galaxy 85

Avocado Coconut Smoothie 86

Matcha Keto Smoothie Bowl 88

Green Smoothie 89

Low Carb Chocolate Almond Smoothie 90

Low Carb Strawberry Crunch Smoothie 91

Chocolate Coconut Keto Smoothie Bowl 92

Chocolate Strawberry Smoothie Bowl 93

Keto Chia Smoothie Bowl 94

5 Minute Low Carb Smoothie Bowl 95

Keto Green Smoothie Bowl 96

Chapter Nine: Keto Breakfast recipes 98

Egg Vegetable Frittata 98

Three-cheese Pizza Frittata 101

Easy Cloud Buns 103

Veggie Frittata 104

Mozzarella Veggie-loaded Quiche 106

Keto Buns 108

BLT with cloud bread 110

Sweet Blueberry Coconut Porridge 112

Avocado and Salmon Low-Carb Breakfast 114

Eggs and Steak 115

Keto Zucchini Breakfast 116

Poached Eggs with Spinach 118

Keto Pancake 119

Swiss chard and Spinach Omelet 121

Cheesy Cauliflower 123

Keto Deviled Eggs 125

Chapter Ten: Fish and Chicken Keto Recipes 126

    Keto fish and chips 126

    Zingy Lemon Fish 129

    Creamy keto fish casserole 130

    Keto fish casserole with mushrooms and French mustard 132

    Keto Thai fish with curry and coconut 134

    Keto salmon Tandoori with cucumber sauce 136

    Low-carb garlic chicken 139

    Keto chicken and cabbage plate 140

    Keto chicken wings with creamy broccoli 141

    Oven-baked paprika chicken with rutabaga 143

    Keto chicken casserole 144

    Keto chicken Garam masala 146

Chapter Eleven: Vegetarian Keto Recipes 148

    Keto white pizza with mushrooms and pesto 148

    Keto grilled veggie plate 151

    Keto Spinach and Goat Cheese Pie 153

    Keto avocado pie 155

    Keto mushroom and cheese frittata 157

    Keto mushroom omelet 159

    Cheese-crusted omelet 160

    Keto smoked mussels' plate 162

    Keto cheese omelet 163

    Oven Roasted Caprese Salad 164

Warm Asian Broccoli Salad 167

Keto Brownie Breakfast Muffins 168

Keto salad 170

Chapter Twelve: Quick Keto Meal Recipes 172

Keto chicken and green beans plate 172

Keto fried halloumi cheese with mushrooms 174

Keto egg butter with smoked salmon and avocado 175

Keto fried chicken with broccoli 178

Keto lamb chops with herb butter 179

Keto Tex-Mex burger plate 180

Keto Caprese omelet 182

Keto ground beef and green beans 184

Keto chicken salad 185

Chapter Thirteen: Keto Snack and Dessert Recipes 186

Keto Flan 186

Keto Butter Pecan Ice cream (Low Carb) 189

Keto Vanilla Pound cake 191

Churro Mug Cake 193

Jicama Fries 195

Tropical Coconut Balls 196

Zucchini Fries with Almond Flour 199

Keto Peanut Butter Cookies 201

Eggplant Chips with Herbs and Olive Oil 202

Keto Parmesan Crisps with Tomato Slices 204

Mini Low Carb Cheesecakes with Blackberry 205
Peanut Butter Caramel Milkshake 207
Conclusion **208**

Introduction

We want to thank you for purchasing this book, "Keto Diet for Beginners."

Can eating fat help me lose weight? Are butter and cheese good for my health? Are carbs unhealthy? It was Atkins that was all the rage some time ago and now it is Keto as its replacement. What is so great about this diet? And why is it suddenly becoming a trendsetter in the fitness and health industry?

Yeah, we can hear you saying about how one of your friend's colleagues went on a keto diet and lost a good amount of weight within a couple of months. In fact, we did read an article about how the keto diet can help with various other health benefits apart from weight loss. But what exactly is a Keto diet and how is it better than the other low-carb diets? We mean there are so many low-carb diets out there and why should we believe this one is better?

But maybe it is true! There are many celebrities advertising this new diet, so, can it be true? Kourtney Kardashian, Mama June, Jenna Jameson and Halle Berry – all these stars are vouching for this diet and its effectiveness when it comes to weight loss! We are sure you have heard about the Ketogenic diet or the Keto diet at some point.

So, what is it all about? The Ketogenic diet is an eating pattern that minimizes your carb intake and increases your fat-intake forcing your body to ditch its primary energy source and use fat as its new form of energy. Though the needs of everyone's body slightly differs, the keto diet needs you to consume,

- 5 to 10 percent of the calories from carbs
- 15 to 30 percent of the calories from protein
- 60 to 75 percent of the calories from fat

When you continue following this new eating pattern, your body enters a state known as ketosis after three to seven days (approximately).

What is ketosis? Ketosis is a metabolic state where your body uses stored fat instead of glycogen (stored glucose) to produce energy. This is when your body produces ketones by breaking up the fatty acids thereby continuing to burn more fat for energy.

You may have a series of questions running through your mind. What are ketones? How will I know if I have entered ketosis? Should I exercise when I am on this dietary routine? Am I doing it right? Where do I get some good and healthy easy-to-make keto recipes?

Well, don't worry! We are going to address most of these questions in this book.

The book will serve as a complete beginner's guide to the readers who want to know more about the ketogenic diet. We will discuss the history of the keto diet and its benefits. We will also discuss how the diet works and what changes you can expect. The chapters in this book will help you understand ketosis. Some chapters in this book have delicious recipes that will help you begin the keto diet the right away!

We hope this book serves as an informative and interesting read to you!

Happy Reading!

Amy Crenn & Suzanne Rodriguez

Chapter One:

Overview of Ketogenic Diet

The Ketogenic diet has gained popularity in the last few years not just for its effective weight loss promise but also for the various other health benefits it provides. The keto diet pushes your body into a state known as ketosis where the body creates a different fuel source (ketones) to provide energy to your body. The primary energy source your body usually uses is the glucose content (from the consumed carbs or the stored carbs).

Your body does not immediately get into ketosis once you start on the ketogenic diet but, instead, it takes several days to do so. This time factor varies from one individual to another! Since the body produces ketones when you follow this diet, the diet is known as the ketogenic or keto diet. Your body is in the ketosis state if the blood ketone levels are more than 0.5mM. It is also possible to achieve ketosis by consuming ketone-related supplements such as MCT oils, HVMN Ketone, Ketone salts, etc., that can raise your blood ketones level.

When you limit your protein and carb intake, your body turns to the stored fats for energy thereby resulting in ketone production. Restricting carbs is to curb glucose production, but why should you reduce your protein intake? Increased intake of protein can lead to a process known as gluconeogenesis where the body produces glucose from various non-glucose molecules like glycerol, protein or lactate.

Since there are various low-carb diets, people often confuse keto with any similar low-carb diets. But just because a diet involves low-carb intake does not necessarily mean it is keto. The differences in the consumption of the macronutrients will help you to determine if the diet is really a ketogenic diet. What are the macronutrients? Macronutrients are crucial essential nutrients consumed by humans in massive quantities to provide the required energy to the body cells. The three primary macronutrients are:

1. Carbohydrates

2. Fats

3. Proteins

A ketogenic diet will be high on fat, have moderate quantities of protein and extremely low carbohydrates. The Ketogenic diet comprises of 80 percent fat, 15 percent protein and 5 percent carbohydrates.

Ketogenic diet and its history

Introduction of the low-carb diet

Fasting led certain medical specialists to explore the idea of a ketogenic diet by mimicking the concept of fasting i.e. consume zero calories. Even today, people believe that fasting is the best self-healing medicine for the human body. Fasting comes with a series of benefits and most of them are due to the presence of ketones in the body.

Fasting is known to cleanse the body and soul – both physically and spiritually, and is a technique that human beings have been using for over a thousand years. Almost all the religions and cultures in the world encourage and endorse fasting in one form or the other. Hippocrates, the ancient Greek philosopher, mentioned fasting as the best medicine to heal oneself of sickness. He said – "*All disease begins in the gut.*"

Fasting can put your body into ketosis and people who practiced fasting were not clearly aware of this crucial factor (ketosis)! The ketosis state in your body is the best natural anticonvulsant drug one can ever have. The physicians at the Mayo Clinic discovered this in the early 1900s. Fasting can bring down the frequency of seizures in epileptic patients. But continuous fasting is not practically possible, especially with small children (affected by epilepsy). This is when the physicians noticed an association between fasting and a low-carb diet. The physicians noticed that the epileptic seizures had reduced in frequency. A strict low-carb diet has almost the same effect as fasting for convulsion. When the scientists identified a way to measure the blood ketone levels, they established a connection between the keto diet and fasting. By mid-1900s, they realized that fasting led to ketone production in the body.

Soon medical practitioners began using the low-carb high-fat diet to treat epilepsy in children and adults alike. Apart from controlling seizures, the ketogenic diet has a variety of benefits. The ketogenic diet helps to regulate the insulin levels in the body, and until the discovery of insulin in 1921; people suffering from diabetes followed this diet. William Banting, a British mortician, promoted this diet in a pamphlet named Letter on Corpulence as a weight loss diet after losing weight.

The fall of the Ketogenic Diet

Many considered this diet (low-carb high fat) as a counter-intuitive approach for health maintenance. Even today, many people fear that continuous consumption of high-fat food may lead to high cholesterol levels, obesity, high blood pressure and various other health problems.

An American biochemist, Ancel Keys published an epidemiological study that connected dietary fat as a primary risk factor for heart disease. In this epidemiological study, Ansel studied how the consumption of fats increased the development of heart disease. The cholesterol and blood LDL derived from the dietary fat accelerate the development of atherosclerotic plaque (the body stores cholesterol in the walls of arteries blocking the blood flow). His work was published at the time the then US President Dwight Eisenhower suffered a heart attack.

The President instantly cut his fat intake after the advice from his physician. This gave more power to Ancel Keys' hypothesis and people began to look at nutrition as a crucial factor. This became the reason for a drastic change in the global food policy and its public practice. Following this, the USDA (United States Department of Agriculture) recommended to decrease the intake of dietary fat in their Dietary Goals for Americans and advised people to include a diet based on cereals and grains.

But there was still no clinical evidence to support the diet-heart hypothesis of Keys during that time. There were a couple of large trials conducted to show that decrease in dietary fat can lower the risk of heart disease but they all failed – including the Women's Health Initiative Randomized Controlled Dietary Modification Trial and the Framingham Study.

After the new USDA guidelines to reduce dietary fat, the obesity rate rose as people started adopting the said guidelines. Few medical investigators pitched in and published hypothesis reports which showed that the recent development in health crisis is due to the increased intake of dietary carbs. John Yudkin, the author of the book "Pure, White and Deadly" described this phenomenon. The book spoke about the widespread fear of dietary fats caused by nutritionists and scientists that almost made them overlook the role of starch and sugar in the body.

Comeback of the Low-carb diets

Around the late 1900s, the concept of low-fat dieting made its rounds after Ancel Keys published the diet-heart hypothesis. It was during this time Dr. Robert Atkins came up with his version of the low-carb diet. He published a book Dr. Atkins' Diet Revolution in 1972 that spoke about a specific low-carb diet, which had similar shades of the ketogenic diet. He mentioned how he had treated around 60,000 patients (estimated count) for obesity and its related conditions in his 40 years of practice.

But there were no clinical studies or trials to confirm or validate the diet benefits mentioned by him. Most of his patients reported various side effects when they started with the diet. The side effects were,

- Nausea
- Fatigue
- Dizziness
- Weakness
- Headache

Experts labeled these symptoms as Atkins Flu as the starting phase of the diet was quite uncomfortable for many patients. After his death in 2003, many people started to promote the keto diet for health. It was during this time the Atkins Foundation funded a group of scientists (Dr. Eric Westman, Jeff Volek and Stephen Phinney) to study the Atkins diet and its effect formally. They discovered that a diet that the Atkins diet outperformed a diet based on the 1977 USDA guidelines. With respect to the measured coronary risk factors that included the decreased low-density lipoprotein cholesterol and the total blood saturated FFA alongside increased the high-density lipoprotein cholesterol.

What caused this outcome? It may be because of the reduced carbohydrate and its associated changes in the hormone setup or because of ketones on the body's metabolism. With more people coming out in support of the high-fat low-carb diet, the public perception began to change and the pendulum swung in its favor. Dr. Jason Fung, Professor Tim Noakes and Professor Thomas Seyfried published their work on the keto diet thereby exposing the defects in the diet-heart hypothesis. Speakers and writers such as Robert Lustig, Nina Tiecholtz and Gary Taubes wrote in favor of the low-carb diet.

The influencers exposed how political decisions in favor of high-carb diets led to the criticism of diets like the keto diet. More pieces of evidence pitched in to show the increase in the rate of diabetes and obesity due to the high-carb diet. Multiple studies also suggested that continuous low-fat diets might be harmful to the overall health. It reached its climax point when a recent meta-analysis of data from 18 countries associated with the high-carb intake with an increase in the mortality rate.

People who earlier feared high-fat intake now began to fear high-carb intake and sugar level increase. The last few years saw a considerable increase in people following the ketogenic diet and its growth in popularity. More people have started to adopt this new dietary pattern and online searches corresponding to the ketogenic diet have grown in numbers.

Today, many people follow the ketogenic diet to treat obesity and metabolic disorders. Thousands of people join in large online forums to discuss the low-carb high-fat diet. They share their success stories by sharing their experiences before and after the diet thereby encouraging more people to adopt this dietary routine.

Macronutrients and Micronutrients

As mentioned earlier, the benefits of a ketogenic diet do not restrict themselves only to weight loss but the diet comes with an array of health benefits. The positive reviews for the said diet have considerably increased and this increase in popularity has led researchers and scientists to conduct additional controlled trials to study its long-term efficiency. The primary reason for this diet to aid in weight loss is the decreased appetite, which naturally makes it quite easy to maintain the low-calorie intake. If you over-consume calories, it will prevent the weight loss in your body irrespective of the composition of your macronutrients.

The mass and ratio of a macronutrient defines how much of the macronutrient one can consume. The percentage of each macronutrient in low-carb diets may vary depending on the diet protocol. When it comes to ketogenic diet, the macronutrient composition is as follows,

Macronutrient composition = 5 percent of carbs + 15 percent of protein + 80 percent of fats.

A classic ketogenic diet demands that you consume 20 to 30 g of carbs in a day while the consumption of fat is dependent on the protein and carbs consumption. A few examples of food that are rich in macronutrients are,

- Fats (coconut oil, olive oil, macadamia nuts, avocado, brazil nuts)
- Protein (eggs, cheese, yogurt, milk, chicken, fish)
- Carbohydrates (sweets, sugary snacks, bread, cereals, pasta, potatoes)

Carbohydrates

The dietary carbohydrates also referred to as carbs are responsible for the generation of energy in your body. The human body uses carbs to produce energy. However, experts say that carbs are not the main source of energy. The body can produce energy from dietary fat and protein.

The carb intake is extremely low when you follow a ketogenic diet, which is a complete contrast to the current western diet. People who follow today's modern western diet get their dietary calories from the carbs they consume. When you consume carbohydrates, your body releases insulin and that in turn hinders the production of ketones in the liver thereby making it impossible for the body to get into ketosis. It is therefore important to monitor and control your carb intake when you are on a keto diet. A standard keto diet will recommend you to reduce your carb intake to 5 percent or lower.

A properly planned and well-devised ketogenic diet will have fiber intake as the crucial component along with fats. Fiber is significant to maintain your gut health and to keep you satiated as it increases the food bulk. Including cruciferous vegetables and leafy greens that are rich in fiber is crucial when it comes to a proper ketogenic diet. Your net carb intake will be the total carbs minus the total fiber and it is this metric that will help you review your carb intake.

You need to understand that an increase in fiber intake does not affect your blood ketone levels as well as the blood glucose. Fibers are digestion resistant and can give you a satiated feeling thereby reducing your hunger.

Proteins

Proteins are large molecular components that are composed of long and small chains of amino acids. What are the functions of dietary protein? They are responsible for,

- Glucose conversion through gluconeogenesis

- Charging up the intermediates in various metabolic pathways such as the Krebs Cycle

- To build the functional and structural components of the cells

Although the body can use protein as an energy source, that is not its primary function. It is therefore important to have an adequate balance of protein in your body to maintain the muscle mass while following the keto diet. You need to ensure the calories from protein intake do not exceed 2o to 25 percent or else the gluconeogenesis process from the protein can hinder the production of ketones.

When you start with the ketogenic diet, let your protein intake be somewhere between 0.8 to 1.2 g per kilogram of your body weight. This can help you balance your protein needs against the possibility of excess gluconeogenesis.

Fats

Fat was always on the wrong side of the spotlight. Many people mistook it to be the reason for increased weight and cardiac issues. Fat is the only macronutrient that has triglyceride molecules. The main functionality of fat as a nutrition in your food is to provide you with additional energy levels and compose the key structural and functional parts of your system.

Fat is often confused with nutrient fat. The fat in your cells and the different types of fat molecules available are not the same.

The different fat molecule types are,

- ***Adipocytes*** (Individual cells that store the lipids or fats)

- ***Adipose tissue*** (the tissue that stores the energy as lipid droplets or fats inside the adipocytes (the fat cells). This is the body fat)

- ***Fatty acids*** (Molecules that are composed of carbon atom chains bonded together, with carboxylic acid at one end)

- ***Lipids*** (a generic term used for polar and insoluble biological fat molecules. You have various lipid class molecules that include the phospholipids, mono-, di- and triglycerols, and the cholesterols)

- ***Triglycerides*** (it is a lipid molecule made up of glycerol and combined with three other fatty acid molecules. Glycerol acts as a backbone for the triglycerides)

The ketogenic diet includes several lipid sources. These lipids, once digested, travel through the bloodstream as fatty acids and triglycerides. The body either uses lipids to produce energy or stores them in the adipose tissue. Dietary fat is the fat you consume while stored body fat is the fat (calories) that the body stores as a reserve. The most important energy in a ketogenic diet is the triglycerides where they account for more than 70 percent of the dietary calories.

Fatty acids can be saturated or unsaturated – a saturated fatty acid will not have any double bonds between the carbons while an unsaturated fatty acid will have one or more double bonds between the carbons. Saturated fats such as coconut oil, butter, etc. are stable and can be in their solid state at room temperature. During the earlier days, dietary unsaturated fats led to the development of high blood pressure and heart disease, so the intake of such fats was either prohibited or limited.

Unsaturated fatty acids can be divided as follows:

- Monounsaturated fats (it has only one double bond between the carbons)

- Polyunsaturated fats (it has multiple double bonds between the carbons)

The behavior of the fatty acid is determined based on the number of double bonds it holds. These fatty acids are mostly in a liquid state at room temperature (example: olive oil). People initially believed that unsaturated fats were healthier than saturated fats, but experts say that saturated fats are healthy fats. Your blood biomarkers (lower blood triglycerides) improve with consumption of monounsaturated and polyunsaturated fats. It is important that you consume adequate unsaturated fats when on a keto diet. An increase in fat intake does not causes cardiovascular issues.

Your body metabolizes the fats based on the length of the chain. The body absorbs the long-chain fatty acids and transfers them to the lymphatic drainage system after which the fatty acids move into the bloodstream. But this does not happen with short-chain fatty acids and medium-chain fatty acids. They do not go into the lymphatic system but travel to the liver directly from the gut via the bloodstream. If you deliver massive amounts of these short-chain and medium-chain fatty acids to the liver all at once, it can trigger the liver to convert these fatty acids into ketone bodies.

Medium-chain fatty acids found in coconut oil are highly ketogenic. But a few people might experience an upset stomach when they consume a large amount of medium-chain fatty acids. So these people will not be able to raise their ketone levels artificially. When you summarize all these concepts, you will be able to understand that you need to increase your dietary fat intake to the maximum to achieve ketosis. Ensure you include a variety of healthy fat from different plant sources such as nuts, coconut oil, avocados, olive oil, etc.

On the contrary, the micronutrients are equally important must be acquired from the diet in minimum qualities. Minerals and Vitamins are the common examples of micronutrients.

Micronutrients in a Keto diet

Sodium, magnesium, potassium and calcium are the important micronutrients that should go into your body during a keto diet. You need to be conscious of your micronutrient intake for the following reasons:

- When you reduce your carb intake, you might have to lower the consumption of various other foods that are rich in micronutrients. Example: Vegetables and fruit

- A few nutrients (sodium, magnesium, potassium, calcium) might go off-balance in your body during the initial 28 days of your keto diet, as most of these nutrients go out of your body as urine or sweat and the frequency of the excretion increases. Your body resolves the issue naturally after it gets adapted to the diet.

- You should increase your intake of sodium since you will lose more extracellular fluid due to frequent urination. The basic functionality of Sodium is to maintain the water balance, blood volume and cell membrane potential. It is also important for nerve conduction and acid-base balance.

During the initial stages of the keto diet, your sodium levels might show a slight dip and it is therefore important for you to add extra sodium to your meals by including more salt. This can also reduce the common side effect of the keto diet – muscular cramps that are mostly associated with low sodium.

The fundamental functionality of Potassium, which is the principal cation in the intracellular fluid, is mostly associated with:

- Electrical activity in cells (cardiomyocytes and neurons)
- Cell membrane potential.

Similar to sodium, the potassium levels also fall due to increased excretion and it is therefore necessary for you to add in more dark green vegetables, avocados and nuts to your keto diet.

The other important element is Magnesium, which plays a major role in immune, nerve and muscle function. Magnesium levels fall due to the increased excretion at the beginning of the keto diet.

You rarely come across a calcium deficiency on a keto diet as your regular intake of leafy greens, cheese and various similar staples can keep your calcium in control. Calcium is crucial for your bone health as well as muscle contraction along with cardiovascular wellness.

Chapter Two:

What Exactly is a Ketogenic Diet?

As mentioned in the last chapter, patients with epilepsy followed the ketogenic diet to reduce the frequency of seizures. It had nothing to do with weight-loss initially. Experts say that ketone bodies and decanoic acid (another chemical generated by the diet) reduce or minimize the frequency of epileptic seizures.

People following the ketogenic diet noticed a decrease in their overall body weight. Experts conducted further research and clinical trials to understand the ketogenic diet better. They found that,

- When you eat carbs, your body tends to retain the fluid to store the carbs as a reserve for energy (just in case your body needs it in future)
- Now when you minimize or eliminate the carb intake, this fluid does not have much usage and you get to lose this water weight.

People often overeat when they consume a large proportion of carbohydrates. When you follow a high-carb diet, you eat more since you always crave for food. However, when you consume a high fat diet, you feel full and your cravings reduce. When you are on a ketogenic diet, your body depletes its entire carb reserves and looks for an alternate energy source. Your body shifts into ketosis and targets the stored fat to produce energy thereby reducing your body weight.

People started to accept this new low-carb high-fat diet because the diet protocol made sense to many. Most people will want to lose some fat from their body to achieve their goal weight and this diet does exactly that by converting the stored fat to a fuel source.

What is Ketosis and how does it work?

The Ketogenic diet, commonly known as the keto diet, is a dietary protocol that expects you to focus on increasing your fat intake and eliminating or reducing the carb intake. This will push your body to a certain metabolic state known as ketosis. The moment your body enters into the ketosis state, it converts the stored fat to fuel and burns it to provide energy to your cells.

So when you are in ketosis, your body burns the stored and dietary fat for fuel and eventually you get to your goal of losing weight, getting healthy, looking good and feeling lighter!

For this to happen, your body should exhaust all the glycogen (stored glucose – sugar) reserves from your body. How do you make this happen?

- You can put your body into the ketosis state when you undergo a complete fast i.e. you do not eat anything at all thereby giving no calories to your body. When this happens, your body does not get any new glucose and therefore turns to its reserve – glycogen (stored glucose). It depletes the entire glucose stores and then starts looking for an alternate energy source. This is when it focuses its attention on the stored fat thereby burning it to produce ketone bodies for fuel.

- Another way to put your body into ketosis is by mimicking fasting. You should deprive your body of glucose by eliminating any food that the body can convert into sugar. This is possible when you increase your fat intake and reduce or eliminate your carb intake. In other words, you are depriving your body of glucose thereby forcing it to look for an alternate energy resource – fat.

When you look at a typical American diet, you will find that it has more than 50 percent carbohydrates. This is the reason why more than 60 percent of the country is obese or overweight. When you replace the carbs with another fuel source, you start to burn fat. Eliminating the carbs or reducing the intake of carbs drastically can make this happen! A ketogenic diet implies a dietary approach, which is high in fat, moderate in protein intake and has minimal to no intake of carbohydrates.

How do you turn your body into a fat-burning machine? When you practice fasting for an extended period or when you consume foods that adhere to the ketogenic diet protocol, your body gets into ketosis thereby forcing it to burn all the stored fats for fuel.

One more important thing is when you eat carb-rich foods your body produces insulin to manage the glucose (sugar) increase in your bloodstream. So naturally, when you reduce the consumption of carbs, the insulin production reduces making your body more insulin sensitive. This comes with a series of health benefits.

So, when your body shifts into ketosis, you not only lose weight, but also experience,

- Lower insulin levels
- Increased energy
- More physical potential
- Increased cognitive ability and brain function

What are Ketones?

So, what exactly are these ketones and where do they come from? As mentioned earlier, when your body exhausts its glucose reserves (glycogen), it will look for another alternative energy source. This is when it gets digging into the body's fat storehouse as stored fat can help to fuel the required energy for your cells.

Since there is no glucose in the body, your liver will take in the stored fats and convert them into fatty acids. These fatty acids are then broken down into functional compounds known as ketone bodies (otherwise known as ketones). Your body uses these ketones to provide energy to your body cells and brain cells. The best part is, when your blood ketone levels increase your appetite decreases. The reason for improved energy is that your brain uses a different source to produce energy.

Your liver generates three different types of ketone bodies,

- Acetoacetate
- Beta-Hydroxybutryate
- Acetone

Your body can fuel itself from ketones in two different ways:

- Your body is capable of making its own ketones when you fast or when you increase your fat intake and reduce your carb-intake forcing the abstinence of glucose
- You can also feed your body with actual ketones by consuming exogenous ketones (ketone supplements)

When your body is on a ketogenic diet, it acts as a fat-burning machine as it switches its primary energy source from glucose to stored fat. This naturally leads to low insulin levels and the fat burning power increases as accessing the fat stores becomes easy. Your body is in ketosis when it produces ketones, and the fastest way to shift your body into ketosis is by fasting. But it is impossible to fast forever, and this led to the development of the ketogenic diet.

Is it possible to lose weight because the body enters into ketosis?

When your body begins to burn stored fat into ketones, your body shifts into ketosis. But why will that make me reduce weight? I understand where you are coming from. Let me explain this to you with an example.

Imagine you have stored a pile of coal for the upcoming winter. When it is winter, you scoop up some of these coal piles into the furnace for heat. As you continue to use up all the coal, the pile gets smaller. Similarly, in ketosis your body burns the stored fat in your body and as it continues to utilize the stored fats (which is your extra flab, water weight, excess calories, etc.), you get smaller i.e. you reduce weight. The coal is the stored fat here and the heat you receive in winter is your energy.

There are numerous studies on how a well-planned ketogenic diet has helped countless people to lose weight and improved their overall health condition by improving their health markers. Another important reason for losing weight on the ketogenic diet is – thermodynamics! When you are practicing the keto diet, you are getting rid of one major macronutrient – carbohydrates!

The following list includes the food items that are rich in carbohydrates.

- Soda

- Bagels

- Fruit smoothies

- Bread

- Sugar candies

- White rice

- Pasta

These foods have a high caloric value, and when you overeat, these carbs are stored in your body as fat. When you restrict or eliminate these carb-rich foods, you consume fewer calories. When you burn more calories than you consume, you lose weight. This is one main reason that most calorie-restricted diets result in weight loss when done right regardless of the proportion of food you consume. On this type of diet, you are not concentrating on the body composition, food quality or muscle synthesis but it is more to do with the amount of food consumption (smaller portions of food).

When your body gets adapted to the keto routine, you feel satiated with fewer calories, which ultimately results in quicker and easier weight loss. But remember, if you overeat on a keto diet, you will definitely gain more weight. So do not expect to lose weight after eating 6000 calories of bacon, beef and butter regularly! You should know how to eat healthy!

The ketogenic diet not only help with weight loss but also aids in,

- Epilepsy treatment
- Type 2 diabetes
- Managing PCOS (Polycystic ovary syndrome)
- Treats acne
- Showing improvement in neurological diseases such as MS (multiple sclerosis and Parkinson's)
- Reducing the risk of cardiovascular and respiratory diseases

Scientists are conducting more research to understand how the keto diet affects patients with Alzheimer's and similar health conditions.

Types of Ketogenic Diets

There are different types of ketogenic diets and each of these come with their own versions of the dieting protocol. But the generic and popularly known types are,

Standard Ketogenic Diet (SKD)

This ketogenic diet type comprises of extremely low-carb, moderate-protein and high-fat diet which typically contains 5 percent carbs, 15 to 20 percent protein and 75 to 80 percent fat.

Cyclical Ketogenic diet (CKD)

This diet comprises of five ketogenic days, which are followed by two high-carb days – it is referred to as higher-carb re-feeds

Targeted Ketogenic diet (TKD)

You can add carbs around your workout schedule and this diet allows you to do that.

High-protein Ketogenic diet

This diet is similar to your standard ketogenic diet but the only difference is in the ratio of the macronutrient composition. The diet includes more protein where the ratios are mostly 5 percent carbs, 35 percent protein and 60 percent fat.

Extensive studies have been conducted on the standard and high-protein ketogenic diets. However, the targeted ketogenic diet and cyclical ketogenic diet are advanced methods of the keto diet that bodybuilders or athletes follow.

When people refer to the ketogenic diet, they usually refer to the standard ketogenic diet in general.

Is Ketogenic diet for everyone?

The Ketogenic diet or the keto diet is not suitable for everyone. Experts suggest that people with certain medical conditions should not follow the keto diet.

Anyone with one or more of the following medical conditions should not get into ketosis,

- Kidney Failure
- Fat digestion disorders (pancreatitis, gallbladder disease, gastric bypass)
- Genetic metabolic defects
    - Beta-oxidation defects
    - Fatty acyl dehydrogenase deficiency
    - CPT I/II deficiency
- Pregnancy
- Liver functional disorders

Side-effects of the Ketogenic diet

When you start with the keto diet, you will feel weak and exhausted for the initial two to three days, as your blood glucose levels are low. Either your body is yet to enter into ketosis mode or the ketone production has not reached a stage where it can provide enough fuel to your brain and body. This particular state of your body can lead to a series of potential side effects. These side effects lead to keto flu, and the common symptoms are:

- Fatigue
- Headache
- Muscle cramps
- Dizziness
- Nausea

If the food you consume does not give your body the required amount of macronutrients and micronutrients, you tend to develop other symptoms that are ahead of the keto flu.

Certain other symptoms that people experience after the adaptation period are,

- Hair loss
- Constipation
- Elevated cholesterol levels
- Increase in blood triglycerides
- Bad breath
- Gallstones
- Exhaustion and tiredness that makes it difficult to maintain your physical performance

You will need to provide your body with adequate micronutrients and enough calories to overcome these symptoms. When you reduce the vegetable and fruit consumption in a keto diet because of the high-carb content, you are not consuming enough fiber content, which leads to vitamin deficiency. It is also possible for the keto diet to alter the way your kidneys work – they may excrete more electrolytes such as sodium and potassium. In such cases, you need to include supplements to reduce the imbalance of the electrolytes in your body.

Your keto diet is more effective if your carb intake is extremely low – a strict keto diet will want you to consume less than 20 grams of net carbs in a day.

How can you enter ketosis effectively?

Some methods you can use to increase the blood ketone levels are,

- Do not consume anything more than 20 g of digestible carbs in a day. You can have more fiber but your carb intake should be strictly restricted.

- Your protein should be on moderate levels. You need to give your body the required amount of protein but nothing more! Try to stay below one gram of protein per kg of your body weight for a day. For instance, if your body weight is 80 kg, then your intake of protein for the day should be 80 grams.

- Eat healthy high-fat foods to keep yourself satiated for the rest of the day. When you plan your diet well, your appetite level will decrease since you feel full with smaller portions of food. Adding more coconut oil, olive oil, etc. should help!

- Do not snack when you are not hungry. Avoid eating for fun or eating when you are bored or eating because you have food in vicinity. More intake of food can reduce the ketosis process and slow down your weight loss routine. If you seriously want to snack because you feel hungry, choose keto-friendly snack items

- If possible, include intermittent fasting to your keto dietary approach. Example, reduce the eating window to 8 hours and increase the fasting window to 16 hours. You can skip your breakfast and have your first keto meal at 11 a.m. and continue with your other meals until 6 p.m. – maybe first meal at 11 a.m., late lunch around 3 p.m. and early dinner by 6 p.m. This combo can help to boost your ketone levels; accelerate the weight loss and reverse type 2 diabetes.

- Include physical activity to your daily routine. Walking, jogging, yoga or any similar simple workout routine should do!

- Have a good and sound sleep – minimum 7 hours to maximum 9 hours. Sleep deprivation can lead to severe stress as the stress hormones go up leading to an increase in the blood sugar levels. This ultimately slows down the ketosis process and hinders the weight loss objective.

Chapter Three:

What to Eat and What not to Eat

The Keto nutritional strategy is to consume high fat, moderate amounts of protein and minimal carbs. This will help your body enter into the ketosis state thereby resulting in the production of the ketone bodies. Your body will soon turn into a fat-burning machine, helping you achieve your goal weight.

Remember, fat is an essential macronutrient that plays a major role in the ketogenic diet and it is not the fact that actually makes you fat!

What to eat?

It is important to begin your diet with natural and whole single-ingredient foods. You can include any or all of the following food items to your keto food list.

Vegetables that grow above the ground

When you include vegetables in your diet recipes, you are free to use either fresh veggies or the frozen ones. The best way to get some good fat into your body on a keto diet is by including vegetables – the ones that grow above the ground. You can choose,

- All the leafy green vegetables
- Cauliflower
- Broccoli
- Cabbage
- Zucchini
- Avocado

- Bell peppers
- Mushrooms
- Asparagus
- Peas
- Beans (Green, black)
- Tomatoes
- Lettuce
- Kale
- Cucumber
- Brussels Sprouts
- Celery
- Eggplant
- Artichokes

You can cook the vegetables with olive oil or coconut oil or butter and allow more healthy fats to get into your system. When you are preparing a vegetable salad, you can use olive oil for dressing. Veggies are your best fat-delivery system, which can add more flavor, color and variety to your keto diet meals.

You will end up eating more vegetables on your keto diet, as you will need to replace your rice, potatoes and pasta with mixed vegetables.

Other Vegetables

You can also include other vegetables such as,

- Onions
- Garlic

- Ginger
- Radish
- Turnip

Healthy Fats

Avocados, seeds and nuts are the key food items that are rich in healthy fats. When you choose nuts, use fewer amounts of cashews, as they are high in carbs. Always go for,

- Pecan nuts
- Macadamia nuts
- Almonds
- Brazil nuts
- Walnuts

You can also include nut butters to your food list. But when you are snacking on nuts, then you need to be a bit careful, as you tend to eat more than you need to feel satiated.

Seeds are also good sources of healthy fats. Include many seeds to your keto recipes,

- Pumpkin seeds
- Pistachios
- Chia seeds
- Flaxseeds

Healthy oils are a great source of fat for your body,

- Coconut oil
- Olive oil

- Avocado oil

Fruit

You can include a moderate amount of berries to your keto diet,

- Strawberry
- Blackberry
- Raspberry

Blueberries have more carbs so be careful when using them – use one or two occasionally.

A few other fruits that you can choose to include in your keto diet are,

- Plum
- Cherries
- Peach
- Mandarin
- Cantaloupe
- Kiwi
- Lemon
- Coconut (the white fleshy thing – the meat of the coconut)

Meatless Proteins

If you are planning on a complete vegetarian or a vegan keto diet, then you can include the following meatless options,

- Seitan
- Tempeh

- Tofu

Condiments

You can include the following condiments to your keto diet plan,

- Pepper
- Herbs
- Salt
- Spices
- Horseradish
- Aioli

Meat

You should avoid processed meats. It is important that you choose unprocessed meats, as they are mostly keto-friendly and contain fewer carbs. If you want to go for the healthiest option, you need to choose grass-fed and organic meat. But since keto diet is high in fat and not in protein, you do not have to add huge amounts of meat to your diet plan.

When you consume more meat, then you end up with excess protein, which is actually more than your body needs. This will push your body out of ketosis as the gluconeogenesis process takes place - converting your proteins into glucose. So, a small to moderate quantity of meat is more than enough for you to stick to your ketogenic diet routine.

It is better to avoid cold cuts, meatballs and sausages as all these processed meats often carry added carbs that is not good for your body. Always look for the ingredients when you are buying processed meats (if you have no other choice). Remember, your carb intake needs to be less than 5 percent.

You need to be careful with the amount you consume with the following meats,

- White meat
  - Turkey
  - Chicken
- Pork products
  - Ham
  - Sausage
  - Bacon
- Red meat
  - Steak

Fatty meats are good for keto diets.

Seafood and Fish

Fatty fish are excellent choices for a good ketogenic diet,

- Tuna
- Salmon
- Mackerel
- Trout

Other seafood such as Shellfish is also a good choice for your keto diet

Eggs

You can eat them in any form,

- Boiled eggs

- Scrambled eggs

- Omelets

- Fried eggs (with coconut oil or butter)

When you buy eggs, go for omega-3, pastured or free-range eggs (eggs that come from free-range animals). Always choose the organic option! Considering the cholesterol content in the eggs, you should not be eating more than 36 eggs in a day. But if you can eat fewer eggs, good for you! When you are making keto-friendly egg recipes, try to add as much unprocessed cheese and butter as possible. It is better to stick to blue, cheddar or mozzarella cheese.

High-fat Sauces, Natural Fat

As mentioned earlier, when you are on a keto diet most of your calories will come from fat and it is therefore important for you to choose the natural source of fat. Eggs, meat, fish and seafood are fat-rich food items but it is also important for you to add more fat to your dishes by cooking in coconut fat, olive oil, coconut oil, butter, etc. You can also include high-fat keto-friendly sauces, dips and spreads such as,

- Garlic butter

- Béarnaise sauce

- Yellow mustard

- Dijon mustard

- Sriracha mayonnaise

- Full-fat mayonnaise

- Buffalo hot sauce

- Creamy salad dressings

- Pesto

- Alfredo sauce
- Chimichurri
- Nacho cheese sauce
- Tzatziki
- Low-sugar BBQ sauce
- Guacamole
- Herbed butter

High-fat dairy products

Until now, you have seen people going for low-fat cheese, low-fat butter, etc. when you are on your weekly grocery shopping. But in your case, you will have to go for the opposite! The keto diet requires you to add in as much healthy high-fat products as possible and high-fat dairy is one affordable choice. You can include,

- Heavy cream (for cooking)
- Grass-fed cream and butter
- High-fat unprocessed cheese
    - Cheddar
    - Mozzarella
    - Blue
    - Goats cheese (optional)
- High-fat yogurts (don't over-eat)

You can use milk sparingly in your coffee as the milk sugar can add up to your carb figure. No cafe latte, please! Do not snack too much on cheese when you are not hungry as it might hinder your weight-loss plan.

Drinks that are allowed

Water is the first option for everyone irrespective of whether you are dieting or not. You need to drink an adequate amount of water to keep your body hydrated. A properly hydrated body will do its work without any hiccups! Coming back to the keto diet, you can have,

- Plain water

- Sparkling water

- Iced water

- Hot water

- Natural flavored water (adding limes, sliced cucumbers or lemons to your water)

- Salted water (add half to one teaspoon of salt to your drinking water if you are suffering from keto flu symptoms or headaches)

You can drink *Coffee* if you do not add sugar, cream or milk to it. But if you are not used to black coffee, you can add a bit of cream or a small amount of milk. You can also make your coffee into a fat-energized drink by adding in coconut oil and butter. You have the bulletproof coffee option too! And do not forget to cut back on your cream, fat or milk in your coffee if you feel a lag in your weight-loss timetable.

Tea is another good option in a keto diet but again no sugar here too. You can go for the following choices of tea,

- Herbal tea

- Black tea

- Green tea

- Mint tea

- Orange Pekoe tea

Bone broth is yet another drink you can consume on the keto diet. This drink is not only satiating but is also full of electrolytes and nutrients that can keep your body hydrated for hours together. It is easy to make and you can add some coconut oil or butter to it for the extra energy quotient

Vegetable stock is also nutritious similar to your bone broth. You can make a simple and nutritious stock from mixed vegetables (add more onions and garlic for the extra-bit of taste)

What not to eat?

You should avoid some food types when you follow the ketogenic diet. The following list of food items should be neither in your kitchen racks nor on your grocery shopping lists.

Sugar

Sugar is the biggest enemy for your keto diet. Get rid of all the energy drinks, soft drinks and vitamin water from your refrigerator – they are all nothing but sugared water. You also need to avoid fruit juice as they have high sugar content. You should be saying a big fat NO to the following list,

- Candy
- Cookies
- Sweets
- Donuts
- Cakes
- Breakfast cereals
- Frozen treats
- Chocolate bars

- Maple syrup
- Agave nectar
- Honey
- Artificial sweeteners (avoid or limit the usage)
- Smoothies
- Ice creams
- Sugary snacks

When you are buying dressing, condiments, packaged food products, drinks and sauces, do check the label for the carb content and hidden sugars.

Starch

You need to avoid the following carb-rich foods, as they are rich in starch and other not-so-keto-friendly contents,

- Rice
- Bread
- Pasta
- Corn
- Potatoes (sweet potatoes as well) – limited amount should be ok
- Muesli
- Potato chips
- Porridge
- French Fries
- Wholegrain products

You may have seen lentils and beans in the "can eat" food list but you should not overeat them as that may lead to carb overload.

You do have keto-friendly bread, pasta, rice and porridge as replacements.

Beer

Beer, also called liquid bread, is rich in carbs. You have too many quickly absorbed carbs in it. Do not worry; you do have a couple of lower-carb beer options! Check this out - https://www.dietdoctor.com/low-carb/keto/alcohol-guide#beer

Fruit

Apart from the fruit that has been mentioned in the can-eat list, you will have to avoid the others! Fruit naturally has high sugar content (fructose) so eating them occasionally when you are on a keto diet is fine.

Margarine

Margarine is not butter – it is imitation butter produced by the food industry. It is rich in high content of omega-6 fat, which is abnormal. It is unhealthy and does not taste good! Margarine is related to various diseases such as allergies, asthma and inflammatory disorders.

Tubers and Root vegetables

Apart from potatoes and sweet potatoes, you will also need to avoid,

- Parsnips
- Carrots (limited quantity is fine)
- Celery root

- Beets

Processed food

You will need to get rid of all possible processed food from your keto diet plan,

- Low-fat diet products (highly processed and rich in carbs)
- Unhealthy fats (refined oils, processed vegetable oils, mayonnaise, low-fat butter, canola oil, etc.)
- Sauces and Condiments which contain sugar or unhealthy fat
- Alcohol (most of the alcoholic beverages are high in carbs and can throw you out of ketosis in no time)
- Sugar-free diet foods (they contain high sugar alcohols that can disturb your ketosis state. They are also highly processed)

Other Keto-approved food that you can hog on

You can go ahead and eat the following keto approved healthy snack items or use them as ingredients for the keto snacks. But I repeat, indulge in snacking only if you are truly hungry between your meals.

- A handful of seeds or nuts
- Cheese (couple it up with olives)
- Dark chocolate (90 percent – better to eat the ones that don't have any form of milk content in it)
- One or two hard-boiled eggs
- Strawberries with cream
- Low-carb milkshake (almond milk + nut butter + cocoa powder)

- Full-fat yogurt (blend it with cocoa powder and nut butter)
- Celery with guacamole and salsa
- Small portions of left-over meals

Grocery Shopping Lists

It is quite common to get intimidated when you are going to start a new diet. Most often people are confused and have no clue about where to start – a common starting trouble! The first step to any diet routine is,

- Listen to your body and understand what it wants
- Research what is needed to improve your current health condition
- Focus on the overall wellness

Your grocery-shopping list should only include food that adheres to the keto diet rules. So, remember to remove carb-rich foods from your kitchen cabinet and refrigerator. All the processed foods, starchy vegetables, sugar, grains, bread, natural or artificial sweeteners and sugar-rich drinks should leave your kitchen space.

When you start the ketogenic diet, you should include the following protein and produce on your grocery list. You can decide the quantity of the shopping list based on your week's plan and do not hesitate to invent your own recipes!

Proteins

- Tempeh
- Chicken breast/legs
- Beef or pork
- Eggs

- Plain goat milk yogurt

Staples needed in your kitchen

- Coconut cream
- Coconut aminos
- Cocoa powder
- Vanilla extract
- Almond flour
- Almond butter
- Peanut butter
- Monk fruit extract
- Almond milk (or any preferred nut milk)
- Coconut milk

Oils and Spices

- Coconut oil
- Olive oil
- Salt (preferably sea salt)
- Pepper
- Ground ginger or ginger powder
- Garlic powder
- Cinnamon powder

Foods rich in Omega-3 fatty acids

- Hemp seeds
- Flax seeds
- Algae
- Chia seeds
- Cod liver oil
- Salmon
- Grass-fed butter
- Sardines
- Egg yolk
- Grass-fed beef
- Walnuts

Dairy products

- Cream cheese
- Cheese (preferably blue cheese, cheddar or mozzarella)
- Sour cream
- Heavy whipping cream
- Salted butter (preferred)
- Greek Yoghurt (Plain)
- Cottage cheese

Keto-friendly sweeteners (one or two of them)

- Monkfruit
- Stevia
- Swerve
- Erythritol
- Allulose
- Truvia
- Sucralose
- Saccharin
- Aspartame

Vegetables

- Mushrooms
- Cabbage
- Cauliflower
- Broccoli
- Brussels sprouts
- Onions
- Spinach
- Celery
- Green beans
- Lettuce
- Asparagus
- Peas

- Beets (use fewer quantity)
- Kale
- Radishes or turnips
- Garlic
- Artichokes
- Okra
- Tomatoes
- Cucumbers
- Bell peppers
- Eggplant

Fruit

- Berries (choose the keto-friendly berries like strawberry, blackberry, raspberry)
- Avocado
- Olives
- Squash
- Lime
- Lemon

Chapter Four:

Food Sensitivity

When you have difficulty in digesting a specific food item, then you have a food sensitivity or food intolerance. Food sensitivity can lead to various symptoms such as,

- Diarrhea
- Intestinal gas
- Abdominal pain or
- Stomach Bloating

Food allergy is often confused with food intolerance but both are different. When there is a problem with your immune system, you get food allergies whereas food sensitivity involves the digestive system. When you have a food allergy, consuming even a tiny amount of allergic food can lead to life-threatening or severe reactions known as anaphylaxis. The symptoms of food allergies are,

- Vomiting
- Skin rash
- Nausea
- Facial swelling
- Breathing difficulty
- Going into a state of shock

How would you know if you are allergic to a food? When you consume a specific food item, your body will show visible reactions in the way it reacts to the food. The immune system is involved here! The reaction will be immediate in most cases. You can see an urgent reaction in your body such as,

- Hives
- Wheezing
- Throat closing

Sometimes, the reactions can be chronic such as,

- Asthma
- Sinusitis
- Eczema
- Flushed cheeks

When such immediate to urgent reactions take place in your body, the body releases histamine causing a systemic reaction. You must identify these quickly since they require immediate medical attention or else it might even lead to fatality.

But when it comes to food sensitivity, the body creates a digestive response and not an immune response. The inability of your body to process certain food items may mostly occur when there is a lack of certain digestive enzymes. Food sensitivity can result in diarrhea, continuous coughing, headaches, etc.

How will I know if I have food intolerance?

Most people are sensitive to dairy products, seafood and nuts. But if you do not really know if you are intolerant to certain foods, you can do a simple test – do not consume any dairy products, seafood as well as nuts for a minimum period of two weeks.

Try this!

- Avoid all the possible offending food such as seafood, eggs, dairy, nuts, soy, peanuts, shellfish, eggplant and mushrooms for 15 days. But it would be better if you can do it for 30 days.

- After you have completed the 30-day period without consuming any of those food items, gradually introduce them into your diet. Eat one serving every day!

- In case you notice any of the following reactions or changes in your body then you might have to avoid that food completely

    - Stuffy nose (food sensitivity)

    - Weight gain (food sensitivity)

    - Red skin, puffy face, severe itchiness (food allergy)

    - Diarrhea (food sensitivity)

    - Gas (food sensitivity)

    - Bloating (food sensitivity)

    - Abdominal pain (food sensitivity)

    - Difficulty in breathing (food allergy)

    - Continuous sneezing (food allergy)

    - Running nose (food allergy)

When it comes to food sensitivity, it is possible to apply a few strategies to help in gut healing.

- Dairy and wheat products can be both allergic and intolerant to a few people. They can damage the gut lining and create a leaky gut. Leaky gut can often cause food sensitivity with foods that you did not have a problem with earlier! So the first step is to ditch the wheat products and dairy products if you are intolerant to these food items. If not, you will never be able to heal your gut issues.

- Glutamine can help your body to rebuild the intestinal lining (gut lining) which has been damaged. Consume 1-glutamine powder twice a day on an empty stomach

- You can also take gelatin or collagen as they work similarly as glutamine.

- Include vegetables that are rich in fiber – soluble fibers are best for healthy guts as it works as a prebiotic! A healthy gut microbiome is crucial for a smooth digestive process.

- If your body usually struggles to digest a food (any food for that matter), it might be due to lack of specific digestive enzymes. Consuming quality digestive enzymes can help your damaged gut by providing the additional support it requires until your gut regains the ability to perform its digestive operation on its own.

- Taking anti-histamines (Vitamin C, quercetin, DAO or bromelain) can be soothing to your body whenever it is suffering from a food reaction. But you need to keep one thing in mind – these natural antihistamines might not necessarily be able to reverse the food sensitivity but can stop the histamine response to the food.

Going dairy-free

How do I go dairy-free when dairy is on everything? The ketogenic diet is about consuming high-fat food and if I do not include dairy, how will I enter ketosis? Today, dairy products are in every single food item – wholesome dairy products (cheese, butter, etc.), snacks (as milk solids), candy (as milk powder), etc. How is it possible to avoid them?

You have no choice but to eliminate dairy from your diet especially if you are intolerant or allergic to it. People who are lactose intolerant have to quit the dairy products completely. If your body shows allergic reactions to any form of dairy, avoid consuming it. But not to worry, there are so many other options available to substitute your dairy products. You can follow a dairy-free lifestyle irrespective of whatever diet you are practicing.

Almost 65 percent of the human population encounters difficulty in digesting lactose after infancy. If you want to know if you are lactose-intolerant, just mix a bit of lactose powder to water and drink it. If you experience digestive issues in 24 hours, then you know your problem!

You can initially begin by mixing 25 g of lactose in water and drink it 3 hours after your last meal or early in the morning. Now that you have consumed lactose, listen to your body and see how it feels. Check if you develop one or more of the following symptoms,

- Flatulence or burping
- Diarrhea
- Abdominal cramps
- Indigestion
- Bloating
- Intestinal pain
- Stomach ache

In case you feel one or more of these symptoms after your lactose drink, then you definitely have a certain degree of lactose intolerance. You will be able to gauge how severe your food sensitivity toward the dairy product is, based on the severity of the symptoms.

You will need to avoid the complete list of the following food items if you have to go dairy-free,

- Half-and-half
- Yogurt
- Butter (in any form – butter oil, butter fat, butter esters, butter acid)
- Cheese (all the animal-derived ones)
- Buttermilk
- Cottage cheese
- Caseinate, Casein hydrolysate, Renate casein and casein (in any form)

- Heavy whipped cream, sour cream
- Pudding, custard
- Tagatose, lactose, lactulose
- Diacetyl
- Milk (condensed, skimmed, dry, evaporated, milk powder, low-fat, malter, non-fat, solid, whole – you have got to give up any milk that is derived from animals (including goat milk))
- Whey protein
- Curd
- Sour milk solids and sour cream solids
- Protein powders made from milk

You should also stay away from any products, listed below, that have milk or dairy products as its ingredients.

- Chocolate
- Baked goods
- Artificial butter flavor
- Margarine
- Caramel candies
- Lactic acid starter culture (and other bacterial cultures)
- Sausages, luncheon meat, hot dogs (they use casein – the milk protein as the binder).
- Nisin
- Nougat
- Any product that contains casein

- Tuna fish (certain brands contain casein)
- Shellfish (check with the seller as some of them dip the fish in milk to lessen the fishy odor)
- Grilled steaks (if you are eating in a restaurant as they add butter for flavor)
- Certain medicines that contain milk protein

If you are lactose intolerant, ensure that you read the ingredients list and avoid foods that may contain milk solids.

Always read the labels and check the ingredients to be extra careful. Be conscious when you are eating out. Question the seller if you are not sure of a particular ingredient.

However, when you are following the ketogenic diet, you do not consume most of the food in the list above. To make it more specific, these are the following products you will come across on a ketogenic diet (and remember you need to avoid all of these):

- Mayonnaise
- Butter
- Heavy whipping cream
- Cheese (soft cheese and hard cheese)
- Half and half
- Greek yogurt
- Spreads (cream cheese, crème Fraiche, cottage cheese, mascarpone, sour cream, etc.)

Dairy-free food that you can consume

You are now clear on what you need to avoid when you need to follow a dairy-free ketogenic diet. It is now time to get started with your dairy-free diet. The following list of food items can be included to your grocery-shopping list:

- Plant-based oils (Olive oil, Coconut oil, MCT oil)

- Animal fats (duck fat, lard, tallow)

- Poultry, seafood, red meat (ensure your red meat consumption is limited). Always go for organic, grass-fed, pasture-raised meat.

- Keto-friendly fruit (Stick to lemon, lime, avocados and berries along with the other fruit mentioned in the previous chapter)

- Vegetables (Include as much as leafy greens, above-ground vegetables and the other veggies mentioned earlier)

- Consume seeds and nuts in moderate quantity. Go for almonds, macadamias, pecans, flaxseeds, pumpkin seeds, chia seeds, etc.

- Replace all your dairy products with non-dairy alternatives (tofu, peanut butter, almond butter, non-dairy curd, non-dairy cheese, etc.)

Look for dairy-free recipes, high-fat vegan recipes or Vegan keto recipes to ensure you are 100 percent into dairy-free meals.

Chapter Five:

Tips and Guidelines

The ultimate objective of a ketogenic diet is to make your body enter into a specific metabolic state known as ketosis. As mentioned earlier, when your body depletes the entire glycogen stores it turns to the fat stores to produce ketones which in turn give energy to the cells in your body. This means, your body's energy source is no more glucose but the ketones.

But there seems to be a problem here – many people who start with the ketogenic diet have a problem in entering into the ketosis state or staying in the ketosis state after they get in! They often push themselves out of the ketosis state. You can overcome this if you avoid the mistakes that amateurs make.

Common mistakes to avoid

Don't be scared of fat

If you want to lose your extra fat then you will have to take in more fat. Does it sound silly? Well, not if you have heard this – "You have to spend money to make money!"

Keto applies a similar logic – your body needs more dietary fat and extremely less dietary carbs to get into ketosis. If you want to change your body to a fat-burning machine, then you should first deprive it of carbs (primary energy source: glycogen – stored glucose). When you do that, your body senses that it has not been getting enough glucose through food and so it starts to use the stored glucose (glycogen). Once it completely exhausts the reserve, it begins to look for an alternate energy source.

Your body targets the stored body fat and breaks it down into fatty acids. These fatty acids produce ketones. When this happens, your body enters into an entirely new metabolic state – ketosis! So, eating more healthy fats is actually going to help you get rid of all the water weight and extra flab. Therefore, you can consume butter and cheese.

Water is important

You need to consistently drink enough water all through the day to keep your body hydrated. The generic advice given by the medical experts is – you need to drink at least one gallon of water every day to help your body's organ to function properly and do its respective job!

It might be hard if you are a working professional but my advice to you is to keep a bottle of clean drinking water next to your workplace. Keep sipping it as often as possible. When you have water near you, you naturally tend to drink more water than you normally do!

You might have to make frequent visits to the restroom but that is fine, as over a period of time your body will get used to your new drinking routine and handle things accordingly.

Get Salty

If you are a first-time keto dieter, you might experience some of the keto flu symptoms. Constant headaches, fatigue, feeling feverish, etc. – but you do not need to worry, you get these symptoms because your body is trying to adapt to a new routine. It is definitely possible to prevent these flu-like symptoms!

You are losing more electrolytes as you are eating real, wholesome food and drinking loads of water. No junk stuff and artificial preservatives are getting into your body. There is a bit of cleansing activity happening in your body – so you have to help your body by refilling the lost electrolytes.

How do you do it? The simplest way to do it is by adding salt (sodium) into your body. You can mix a teaspoon of salt to your drinking water and have it once a day. You can also add sriracha or chili garlic sauce to your food as they have sodium. You can add a bit more salt while you are giving extra seasoning to your salads or other dishes.

There is another benefit in consuming more salt – your body will be able to retain water effortlessly thereby reducing your trips to the restroom!

Dairy is good but don't go overboard

The protocol of the ketogenic diet is to include a large amount of high-fat food items and the most commonly used high-fat food source is – full-fat dairy.

The issue here is, when you consume too much dairy (more than the required calorie amount), you suddenly begin to realize that you have reached a plateau. At this stage, you do not lose any more weight. Why? The theory here is – if you need to lose weight, you need to put your body into a calorie deficit mode i.e. give it fewer calories.

For instance – if your body is burning around 1500 calories daily and you consume 1000 calories, now your body needs to find the remaining 500 calories to burn. When you are in keto, you give that to your body in the form of fat. Coming back to our dairy products – since most dairy items are rich in calories, it is quite natural for you to over-eat resulting in calorie overload. This means – you do not allow your body to burn the extra fat for more energy as you are already feeding it with the required fat.

It is good to add a good amount of mozzarella to your meals but do not eat the entire block of mozzarella in one go.

Know your WHY factor

The important part of any diet is – you should know WHY you are doing it. Are you practicing a particular diet because you want to look good? Or are you doing it to improve your overall health? Whatever the reason is you need to fix it strong in your mind. 99 percent of your diet's success lies in your psychology – your mental capacity should be strong! You need to be sure of why you are doing it and believe that it will work!

You might often get tempted to consume things that will push you out of ketosis. You need to think about your WHY during those times. Your goal, your objective is important! It is okay if you cheat once, do not crib over it. Think positive – ask yourself the question, why should I not get back on track? I can get back on the board and reach my destination soon.

The WHY should motivate you and push you forward to reach your goal. It has a real strong emotion!

Too much protein isn't good

This is another reason for your body to go out of ketosis state. Since you can include meat in your diet, there are times that you often tend to over-eat the meat dishes. Too much protein can produce glucose through the gluconeogenesis process. The body first converts excess protein to glycogen, and converts the glycogen into fat.

Adding chicken breast to your diet routine is good but eating a whole bucket of the chicken fry is probably not going to do any good for your keto diet. Remember to take note of your daily macros to avoid such instances. Otherwise, buy less meat while you go for your grocery shopping!

Stop snacking often

Too much snacking can knock you out of ketosis as it can spike up your blood sugar levels. The good thing with a keto diet is since you include a good amount of high fat to your food you get to feel more satiated. So your temptation to have snacks reduces especially when you have included more fiber to your food platter.

A handful of almonds for energy is good but a bowl of cashews is not! The best way to reduce too much snacking is – to prepare your meal much in advance of your eating time so that you do not indulge in snacking as you cook your meal.

No more habit-eating

Gaining better control over your appetite is one of the best things about the keto diet. Most people listen to their stomach growl and walk toward the refrigerator or pantry in search of something to eat. You should give that habit up to avoid giving into your cravings. You might not experience these things after 2 to 3 weeks of keto dieting.

But few people might experience a hiccup here – since you are eating in a specific way for some time, you get accustomed to that habit. For instance, you might be used to eating something after every three hours and this habit eating will now take you to the refrigerator even when you are not hungry. You need to consciously work toward switching off your mind to this habit. The best way to achieve this is by planning your meals much earlier – meal plan plays an important role in the keto diet.

Sleep is essential

If you are not giving your mind and body the much-required rest, your system is going to face difficulty in doing things it is supposed to do. Good quality sleep is important to control your stress, give rest to your organs and to make you feel energetic the following day.

Eight hours of sleep is mandatory and thankfully following a well-planned keto diet will give you the required sleep without any issues. But if you are a party animal, do not blame me!

Stress management

Over-stressing yourself is going to increase the cortisol levels in your body. What is cortisol? The stress hormone increases your blood sugar level hindering your weight-loss plan.

When your body experiences a consecutive rise and fall in your blood sugar levels, it sends a confusing signal to your brain. Your brain naturally assumes that it is time to refill the glycogen reserve and so it sends you a signal by telling that it needs carbs now! Your body craves for sugar when it is under stress. This is the survival mechanism of the body! If you want to have a successful keto journey, then you need to work on your stress management.

Don't eat the same meal every time

You need to mix up your meals or else you will get bored too soon. There are so many keto-friendly recipes out there and all you need to do is choose the ones that are best for you. You can also discover your own new recipes by adding in your touch of culinary expertise. Add some low-carb veggies to your usual keto meal and spice it up with herbs and condiments.

When there are numerous options available why would you want to eat the same lunch and dinner for the entire month? Unleash your creativity and turn your kitchen into an experimentation lab!

No cheat days

There are few diets which offer you cheat days so that you can wolf down all your favorite stuff on that one day. But beware – there are no cheat days in keto. This is a strict diet routine and you need to adhere to its protocols if you want to achieve your goal weight. If you feel like having a sponge cake or milk chocolate, make a fat bomb and have it.

Keto offers you a substitute for almost everything. Be aware of your mistakes and make preparations accordingly. It is crucial to plan your meals to avoid these commonly repetitive mistakes. Once you get into ketosis, it is not that easy to come out of it but it is not easy to stay on it either!

Quick tips you can follow

Keto is a simple, straightforward diet routine but you need to know the basics before you jump into it.

- How do you cook easy keto meals?

- I have been avoiding fats all these years, how do I get it back to my diet?

- My work routine often forces me to eat out once in a week. How do I manage to stay on keto then?

- How do I start my day on a keto diet?

These common questions might pop up when you are following the diet for the first time. It is quite simple to get started with keto – no complications at all!

- You can consume eggs in any form; however, it is best to add more coconut oil, olive oil and butter while preparing the eggs.

- You do not necessarily need to start your day with a mandatory breakfast. No, it is not really the important meal of the day – breaking the fast (breakfast) is important. So if you are not hungry in the morning, you do not need to eat for the sake of eating. Drink loads of water, have a cup of herbal tea or a cup of coffee. You often experience reduced hunger when you are on keto, so skipping a meal is fine!

- If you are someone who wakes up with a grumbling stomach every morning, not to worry there are tons of easy-to-make breakfast recipes available. You can get hold of a few in this book too!

- Plan your main meals (lunch and dinner) much ahead of time. A simple main course made of meat or fish accompanied by a vegetable side or a salad. Or a super nutritious vegetable main with a healthy smoothie should do the magic!

- If you feel constantly hungry when you start the keto diet, eat more fat and fiber-rich food – eggs, leafy greens, cruciferous veggies, etc.

- If you are out at an official dinner party or a get-together with your friends, replace your pasta or bread with veggie mains + olive oil or butter.

- Go for a fish-based dish or replace the high-carb food with extra mixed vegetables. Try the egg-based meals – scrambled eggs, omelet, fried eggs, etc.

- Choose the burgers without buns and replace your French fries with veggies and add a bit of cheese or guacamole to it

- Mexican dishes offer extra salsa, cheese and sour cream

- Choose berries with cream, mixed cheese board as your dessert option

Chapter Six:

Frequently Asked Questions (FAQs)

Is Keto diet good for everyone? Or are there any restrictions?

Before following any new diet routine, it is advisable to consult your doctor or any trusted dietician to discuss on your nutrition chart.

Pregnant women, nursing mothers and diabetic patients without consulting their physicians, should not practice the Keto diet.

Experts suggest that people with the following conditions should not follow the ketogenic diet since their body should not shift into the state of ketosis.

- Abdominal tumors
- Weakened Fat digestion
- Gallbladder issues or disorders
- Kidney failure
- Weak gastrointestinal motility
- Carnitine deficiency
- Beta oxidation deficiency
- Pancreatitis
- CPT I/II deficiency
- Issues in liver functioning
- Gastric bypass surgery

Can Vegans or Vegetarians follow Keto diet?

Yes! As mentioned earlier, meatless proteins can substitute meat. A Vegetarian Keto diet will include eggs, dairy products, vegetables, greens and legumes.

If you are a vegan, you can remove dairy products, eggs and other animal products. Mushrooms, non-dairy vegan products such as coconut oil, MCT oil, full-fat vegan butter and cheeses will replace the dairy products. For vegetarians and vegans, meatless proteins and various other vegan meat options can substitute meat.

It is, therefore, possible to follow a low-carb high-fat ketogenic diet using a vegan or vegetarian-eating pattern.

Should I be continuing with the Keto diet like forever? Does this mean I cannot get back to eating carbs again?

The ketogenic diet works as long as your body is in ketosis – this is similar to exercising. You lose a good amount of weight using the ketogenic diet and if you go back to your usual routine, you will gain all the weight you lost in the first place. So, you go right back to where you started!

You can follow a ketogenic diet routine for thirty days to check how your body adapts to the routine. When you know your body has adapted to the keto routine and you have achieved your goal (weight loss or reversing a particular health issue), you can slowly include carbs to your food plate.

This will not spike up your insulin levels all of a sudden and the shock does not affect your body either. Reintroduce higher carbs every alternate day or once in a week and slowly increase the level.

If you feel the keto diet does not really work well for your body, it is fine – do not force your body and overexert it. Understand the concept and devise your own diet regimen for a better health and overall wellness.

When can I eat carbs again? Is there a timeline for it?

As mentioned in the answer to the previous question, you can reintroduce the carb food items into your routine slowly and carefully. Eating a high-carb food immediately after your last keto day will spike up your insulin and shock your body. You can probably start eating equal amounts of carb to your diet after two or three months of your ketogenic diet routine.

What if I lose my muscle because of the keto diet?

You might lose some muscle on any particular diet but that will be minimal. But if you are a sportsperson, an athlete, or an individual who gets involved in strength training (lifting weights, etc.), the high ketone levels and the protein intake (you take after your workout) will minimize the muscle loss.

Can I take more protein than fat?

No. If you consume more protein than fat, then it becomes a Paleo diet. Your protein intake should be moderate as too much of protein can lower the ketones and spike up your insulin levels. The maximum protein allowed is 35 percent (in terms of calories).

Why am I always tired or weak? Sometimes I feel I am suffering from severe fatigue. Is it something to be concerned about?

You may experience fatigue and weakness if your body is shifts out of ketosis under stress or pressure. If your body does not burn the fats into ketones, you will be exhausted. You need to check on your carb intake and add MCT oil to your food to get back to ketosis.

Why does my urine smell different? Is there a problem?

No, nothing to worry! This happens when the body does not retain the by-products created during ketosis.

I feel I have a bad breath all of a sudden. Is it because I am doing the diet wrong?

No. You are doing the diet right! Your body reacts this way since it is now in the state of ketosis. It will soon be back to normal in a few days. Drink plenty of water!

Isn't Ketosis dangerous?

Ketosis is not dangerous but ketoacidosis is! A common misconception often happens with the majority of the people. Ketoacidosis occurs due to uncontrolled diabetes but ketosis happens when your body shifts from its primary energy source – glucose to a different energy source - stored fats. The formal is dangerous while the latter is perfectly healthy and normal!

I have diarrhea and digestion problems since I started with this diet. Should I stop the diet?

No, you do not need to quit the diet! Diarrhea, digestion issues, constipation, bowel discomforts are some of the common side effects of the ketogenic diet. You experience these issues for the initial three to four weeks after which it goes off. Include more high-fiber vegetables for smooth bowel movements and add magnesium supplements to manage constipation.

How much weight will I lose when my body stays in ketosis?

There is no concrete number to the amount of weight loss as the results may vary depending on the body composition. But for most individuals, around two to four pounds of weight-loss is possible – and this is partially the water weight. Once the water weight has gone out of the body, you tend to lose around one pound of excess fat every week.

Some people may lose weight faster while some may take a bit of time – usually, young adults (mostly young men) tend to lose weight faster compared to women who have crossed 40 years of age. If you want to speed up the process, you can substitute your oils with MCT oil and take ketone supplements.

The moment your body reaches your normal healthy weight (body weight), the weight loss process will slow down. Your weight eventually stabilizes when you stay on a keto diet but you need to make sure you eat only when you are hungry (no snacking often)

Is there a way to track how much carbs I consume?

Yes! You can do that by using popular apps such as Chronometer or MyFitnessPal

Are you sure that the keto diet is safe on a long run?

Yes, it is safe! But as mentioned earlier, it is best not to follow the keto diet if you are a nursing mother or an expecting mom. You should also avoid this diet if you are taking medicines for high blood pressure. Diabetic patients who are on medication should strictly avoid this diet. But if you do not fall in any of these categories, you can definitely go ahead with the keto diet and it is perfectly safe!

How will I know if my body has entered ketosis or not?

If you see or experience any of the following signs, then it means your body is in ketosis,

- Metallic taste in your mouth or complete dry mouth
- Feeling thirsty always and feeling the need to urinate often
- Bad breath
- Increase in energy levels and a decrease in appetite.

If you still are not sure, you can check your ketone levels by measuring them using any of the three methods,

- Breath analyzers
- Urine strips
- Blood meters

How safe is a keto diet for the kidneys?

People often assume a diet that is high in protein can be dangerous for the kidneys. The point here is the keto diet is not high in protein but fat. And another fact is – an individual with normal kidney function can handle excess protein quite well. So you do not really need to worry about your kidney as a keto diet acts as a shield to your kidneys especially if you are a diabetic.

Chapter Seven:

Lose 20 pounds in 30 days

Is it possible to lose twenty pounds in a month? Yes, it is! But only if you are ready to optimize and make the best use of any of the following three factors:

- Exercise
- Supplement or drug routine
- Proper diet

The Ketogenic diet coupled with a good workout routine can help you achieve your dream weight, which should definitely be your body's healthy weight!

Following the rules

There are a few important rules that you need to take up seriously and follow it to achieve your target weight.

Stay away from all the white carbs

Yes, you read it right! Do not consume any carbohydrate that is white or can possibly be white. Cereal, Pasta, White bread, Potatoes, rice, fried food coated with breadcrumbs – say a big NO to all of these! You should avoid white carbs to ensure that your body does not shift out of ketosis.

Mix and match but eat the same few meals repeatedly

A successful dieter (irrespective of the goal – be it fat loss or muscle gain) will eat a couple of meals repeatedly. You can go for a mix and match routine but you will have to repeat certain ingredients or food items from the following categories:

- Legumes (Pinto beans, Lentils, black beans)

- Vegetables (Mixed vegetables, asparagus, peas, spinach)
- Proteins (Pork, Chicken thigh/breast, egg whites (with a whole egg), Grass-fed organic beef)

You can make any meal from the food items mentioned above but ensure you add as many ingredients as possible to your meal. Do not make your meal complicated – keep it simple! Choose three or four meal recipes and repeat them once or twice in a week. If you happen to dine out, request the restaurant guys to replace the potatoes or French fries with vegetables or salad. Certain Mexican dishes use vegetables in the place of rice and add it to their cuisine list!

Often people who go on a low-carb diet (any diet – can be keto too) talk about quitting because they are not getting enough energy. But the problem here is – they have not consumed the right combination of the food or they consume fewer calories. For instance, when you replace rice with spinach, you need to understand that the calories should be matched accordingly – 1/2 cup spinach = 15 calories while 1/2 cup rice = 300 calories, so it is important that you add legumes to your veggies to load it with enough calories.

If you are looking to tone your body and maintain a good physique, you will definitely be including a strong workout routine along with your dietary approach. In case you are into an intense workout regimen, your food intake is equally important. A sportsperson or an athlete's chart might look something similar as mentioned below:

- Breakfast at 10 a.m.
- Lunch at 1 p.m.
- Healthy snacking at 5 p.m.
- Sports training by 7 p.m. (some may train for 1 to 2 hours)
- Dinner by 9 or 10 p.m.

As mentioned earlier, they also tend to repeat specific meals repeatedly such as,

- Grass-fed organic beef with a lot of mixed vegetables and lentils
- Scrambled eggs with black beans and mixed vegetables
- Chicken or other meat with mixed vegetables, guacamole and pinto beans

Stop drinking calories

You can drink loads and loads of water – even black coffee, black tea, iced tea without sugar is good! But stop drinking carbonated drinks, diet sodas (has many chemical preservatives); soft drinks, milk or fruit juices (the ones with high sugar content). A glass of wine is good to go!

Have a cheat day once in a week (if you want)

You can eat whatever you want once in a week but only if you are combining your diet with strength training. If you are not including exercise to your diet routine, then sorry – no cheat day for you!

<u>Always ensure you include wholesome natural food to your platter</u>

Do not load your plate with store-bought food or eat out continuously. It is true that you can eat high-fat food but that does not mean you should treat your stomach as a dump yard and push in all those unhealthy fats into it. It is always advisable to cook your own meals and stick to the diet routine.

Structured 30-day meal plan

Week One

	Breakfast	Lunch	Snacks or desserts	Dinner
Day 1	5-minute low carb smoothie bowl	Keto Fish and Chips	Keto Parmesan Crisps with tomato slices	Low Carb Garlic Chicken
Day 2	Mozzarella Veggie-loaded Quiche + Blueberry Galaxy	Keto white Pizza with mushrooms and pesto	Keto Peanut butter cookies	Keto chicken wings with creamy broccoli
Day 3	Sweet Blueberry Coconut Porridge + Spinach Avocado Green Smoothie	Keto Avocado Pie	Jicama Fries	Keto Chicken and Cabbage Plate
Day 4	Veggie Frittata + Avocado Coconut Smoothie	Keto mushroom omelet	Keto Butter Pecan Ice cream	Keto salmon tandoori with cucumber sauce

Day 5	Keto Zucchini Breakfast + Avocado Smoothie	Keto Chicken Casserole	Peanut butter caramel milkshake	Keto Spinach and Goat Cheese Pie
Day 6	Low Carb Strawberry Crunch Smoothie	Keto grilled veggie plate	Keto Vanilla Pound cake	Keto fish casserole with mushrooms and French mustard
Day 7	Poached Eggs with Spinach + Low carb Chocolate Almond Smoothie	Keto Thai Fish with curry and coconut	Churro Mug cake	Keto cheese omelet

Week Two

	Breakfast	Lunch	Snacks or desserts	Dinner
Day 1	Egg vegetable frittata + Keto Green Smoothie Bowl	Keto fried halloumi cheese with mushrooms	Keto butter pecan ice cream	Keto Tex-Mex burger plate
Day 2	Avocado and Salmon low-carb breakfast + Matcha	Keto Caprese Omelet	Zucchini fries with almond flour	Keto fried chicken

	Keto Smoothie Bowl			with broccoli
Day 3	Keto Chia Smoothie Bowl	Keto lamb chops with herb butter	Keto vanilla pound cake	Creamy keto fish casserole
Day 4	Cheesy Cauliflower + Green Smoothie	Keto egg butter with smoked salmon and avocado	Eggplant chips with herbs and oil	Oven-baked paprika chicken with rutabaga
Day 5	Egg Vegetable Frittata + Chocolate Coconut Keto Smoothie Bowl	Cheese-crusted omelet	Mini low carb cheesecakes with blackberry	Keto Salad
Day 6	Avocado smoothie	Keto smoked mussels' plate	Tropical coconut balls	Keto ground beef and green beans
Day 7	Sweet Blueberry Coconut Porridge + Keto Green Smoothie Bowl	Keto chicken salad	Churro mug cake	Keto salmon tandoori with cucumber sauce

Week Three

	Breakfast	Lunch	Snacks or desserts	Dinner
Day 1	Veggie Frittata + Avocado Coconut Smoothie	Keto cheese omelet	Churro mug cake	Keto chicken and cabbage plate
Day 2	Green Smoothie	Keto avocado pie	Tropical coconut balls	Low-carb garlic chicken
Day 3	Keto Zucchini Breakfast + Spinach Avocado Green Smoothie	Keto mushroom and cheese frittata	Keto peanut butter cookies	Keto chicken and green beans
Day 4	Blueberry Galaxy	Keto chicken garam masala	Keto parmesan crisps with tomato slices	Keto grilled veggie plate
Day 5	Low carb chocolate Almond Smoothie	Keto mushroom omelet	Peanut butter caramel milkshake	Keto Spinach and Goat Cheese Pie
Day 6	Poached Eggs with Spinach	Cheese crusted omelet	Keto Flan	Keto chicken wings with creamy broccoli

| Day 7 | Easy Cloud buns + Chocolate Coconut Keto Smoothie Bowl | Keto chicken casserole | Jicama fries | Keto cheese omelet |

Week Four

	Breakfast	Lunch	Snacks or desserts	Dinner
Day 1	Cheesy Cauliflower + Low Carb Chocolate Almond Smoothie	Keto egg butter with smoked salmon and avocado	Zucchini fries with almond flour	Keto chicken and cabbage plate
Day 2	Low Carb Strawberry Crunch Smoothie	Keto fried halloumi cheese with mushrooms	Keto Flan	Low carb garlic chicken
Day 3	Keto Zucchini Breakfast + Spinach Avocado Green Smoothie	Keto Zingy Lemon Fish	Keto Vanilla pound cake	Keto fried chicken with broccoli
Day 4	Poached Eggs with Spinach + Avocado	Keto fish and chips	Keto butter pecan ice cream	Keto ground beef and

				green beans
	Coconut Smoothie			
Day 5	Green Smoothie	Keto lamb chops with herb butter	Mini low carb cheesecakes with blackberry	Keto salad
Day 6	Chocolate Strawberry Smoothie Bowl	Keto chicken casserole	Eggplant chips with herbs and olive oil	Keto Tex-Mex burger plate
Day 7	Avocado Smoothie	Keto chicken salad	Jicama fries	Creamy keto fish casserole

Shopping Lists

Dairy and Eggs

- Heavy whipping cream
- Ricotta cheese
- Mozzarella cheese
- Parmesan cheese
- Eggs
- Cream cheese
- Cream of tartar
- Soft goat cheese

- Butter (salted and unsalted)
- Mayonnaise (low carb)
- Herb butter
- Blue cheese
- Feta cheese
- Sour cream
- Mature cheese
- Halloumi cheese
- Mexican cheese
- Salted caramel

Meat and Fish

- Pepperoni
- Smoked salmon
- Sirloin
- Whitefish (salmon, cod, catfish or similar ones)
- Chicken drumsticks
- Chicken thighs or breasts
- Rotisserie chicken (you can make it or buy)
- Chicken wings
- Lamb chops
- Ground beef

Vegetables and Fruit

- Spinach (fresh or frozen)
- Avocado (ripe ones)
- Blueberries (fresh or frozen)
- Goji berries
- Kale
- Strawberries (fresh or frozen)
- Raspberries (fresh or frozen)
- Baby spinach
- Tomato
- Garlic
- Onion (white and red ones)
- Zucchini
- Chives
- Mushrooms
- Parsley (fresh or dried)
- Swiss chard
- Cauliflower
- Rutabaga
- Broccoli
- Scallions
- Capers (small ones)

- Leafy greens (Fresh)
- Cilantro
- Cucumber
- Lettuce
- Bell pepper (green, red, yellow)
- Lime and Lemon
- Cabbage (green)
- Orange
- Cherry tomatoes
- Ginger
- Leek
- Fresh Dill
- Eggplant
- Black olives
- Romaine lettuce, arugula lettuce
- Canned smoked mussels
- Turnip
- Small capers
- Jicama

Herbs and Spices

- Ground Cinnamon
- Italian seasoning

- Salt (normal and sea salt)
- Black pepper
- Cayenne pepper
- Ground cumin
- Chili powder
- Ground nutmeg
- Ground flaxseed
- Garlic powder
- Dried rosemary
- Dried oregano
- Chili flakes
- Dijon mustard
- Dried paprika (+ ground)
- Curry powder
- Curry paste (green or red)
- Tandoori seasoning
- Ground ginger
- Ground turmeric
- Ground coriander seeds
- Ground green cardamom
- Onion powder
- Tex-mex seasoning

- Dried basil
- Allspice powder
- Red chili pepper

Oils and Condiments

- MCT oil
- Coconut oil
- Olive oil (Normal and extra-virgin)
- Nonstick cooking spray
- Avocado oil
- Dill pickle relish
- Green pesto
- Red wine vinegar
- White wine vinegar
- Pickled jalapenos

Baking goods & non-dairy products

- Full-fat Coconut milk (unsweetened)
- Vanilla extract
- Erythritol or powdered stevia
- Coconut yogurt
- Coconut (shredded or grated or flakes)
- Desiccated coconut

- Cacao powder
- Almond butter (salted)
- Unsweetened Almond milk (Plain and flavored)
- Cocoa powder
- Liquid Coconut stevia
- Coconut cream (unsweetened)
- Nutritional yeast
- Almond flour
- Coconut flour
- Maple pecan sweetener
- Swerve sweetener
- Maple extract
- Peanut butter

Nuts and Seeds

- Chia seeds
- Almonds
- Psyllium seeds
- Brazil nuts
- Chopped walnuts
- Hemp seeds
- Pecans
- Sunflower seeds

- Sesame seeds

Others

- Matcha powder
- Cacao Nibs
- Greens powder

Chapter Eight:

Smoothies and Smoothie-bowl Recipes

Strawberry Shake

Servings: 2

Ingredients:

- 1 ½ cups almond milk
- ½ cup coconut milk, unsweetened or heavy whipping cream
- 5 ounces strawberries
- 2 tablespoons sugar-free vanilla syrup
- 2 tablespoons coconut oil
- Whipped cream or coconut cream, to top (optional)
- 2 tablespoons chia seeds (optional)

Method:

1. Place all the ingredients in a blender, and blend until you obtain a smooth mixture.
2. Pour into tall glasses and serve topped with whipped cream if using.

Nutrition Information per Serving:

Calories 276 Kcal (Fat: 27.4 g | Protein: 2.5 g | Net carb: 6.4 g)

Pumpkin Chai Smoothie

Servings: 1

Ingredients

- 1 cup coconut milk (full-fat)
- 2 tbsp pumpkin puree
- 1 tsp chai tea leaves
- 1 tbsp MCT oil (optional)
- 1 tsp vanilla extract
- 1 tsp pumpkin spice
- 1/2 fresh avocado

Toppings

- 1/2 tsp pumpkin spice

Method

1. Add the ingredients, except for avocado, to the blender and blend until you obtain a smooth mixture.

2. Now, add the avocado to the blender and blend until the fruit has broken apart.

3. Pour the smoothie into a glass and top it with pumpkin spice. Drink immediately.

Nutrition Information per Serving:

Calories 399 Kcal (Fat: 32.6 g | Protein: 21.8 g | Net carb: 6.6 g)

Spinach Avocado Green Smoothie

Servings: 2

Ingredients

- 2 cups spinach (cleaned)
- 1 de-stoned ripe avocado (halved)
- 1-cup coconut milk (unsweetened) – use refrigerated cartons and not cans!
- Sweetener, to taste (optional)
- 2 teaspoons vanilla extract

Method

1. Place the cleaned spinach and avocado in a high-speed blender.
2. Add the coconut milk and vanilla extract.
3. Blend on high for one minute until creamy and smooth
4. Add the low-carb sweetener of your choice and blend again (for 30 seconds)
5. Transfer the smoothie into a serving glass. Serve immediately.

Nutrition Information per Serving:

Calories 468 Kcal (Fat: 32.6 g | Protein: 21.8 g | Net carb: 6 g)

Avocado Smoothie

Servings: 2

Ingredients

- 1/2 de-stoned avocado
- 1 cup coconut milk (unsweetened – from carton please)
- 1/4 cup ice
- 1 teaspoon vanilla extract
- Erythritol or Stevia, to taste

Method

1. Place the avocado in a high-speed blender and add the coconut milk
2. Add the ice, vanilla extract and the sweetener into the mixture.
3. Blend on high for 60 seconds until rich, creamy and smooth.
4. Transfer to a glass and serve chilled

Nutrition Information per Serving:

Calories 118 Kcal (Fat: 11 g | Protein: 1 g | Net carb: 2 g)

Blueberry Galaxy

Servings: 2

Ingredients

- ½ cup blueberries
- 2 teaspoons vanilla extract
- 2 cups unsweetened coconut milk
- 2 teaspoons MCT oil
- Stevia, to taste
- 2 scoops whey protein powder

Method:

1. Place all the ingredients in a blender, and blend until you obtain a smooth mixture.
2. Pour into tall glasses and serve.

Nutrition Information per Serving:

Calories 215 Kcal (Fat: 10 g | Protein: 23 g | Net carb: 4 g)

Avocado Coconut Smoothie

Servings: 2

Ingredients

- 1 de-stoned large ripe avocado, chopped
- 1 teaspoon MCT oil
- 1 inch piece ginger, peeled, sliced
- 1 teaspoon shredded coconut (unsweetened)
- 1/2 cup almond milk
- 1 1/2 cups unsweetened coconut milk (from a can)
- 1 tablespoon lime juice or more to taste
- 1 teaspoon turmeric powder
- Stevia to taste
- 2 cups crushed ice.

Method

1. Place the avocado pieces in the high-speed blender.
2. Pour the coconut milk into it and add the MCT oil along.
3. Blend on high for 60 seconds until thick and creamy.
4. Add the lime juice, ginger, turmeric and blend again for 45 seconds.
5. Add ice and blend again.
6. Pour into tall glasses.
7. Serve immediately.

Nutrition Information per Serving:

Calories 208 Kcal (Fat: 21 g | Protein: 1 g | Net carb: 3 g)

Matcha Keto Smoothie Bowl

Servings: 1

Ingredients

- 1 teaspoon matcha powder
- 1 tablespoon coconut flakes
- 1 tablespoon chia seeds
- 8 ounces coconut yogurt
- 1 tablespoon cacao nibs
- 1 tablespoon goji berries

Method

1. Blend together the coconut yogurt and matcha powder on high for 60 seconds until creamy and smooth.
2. Transfer the smoothie into a bowl
3. Top it with coconut flakes, chia seeds, cacao nibs and goji berries
4. Serve immediately and enjoy!

Nutrition Information per Serving:

Calories 420 Kcal (Fat: 28 g | Protein: 13 g | Net carb: 3.1 g)

Green Smoothie

Servings: 2

Ingredients

- 2 cups kale or spinach (washed and cleaned)
- 1 cup unsweetened coconut milk (no cans, only cartons)
- 10 raw almonds
- 1 tablespoon psyllium seeds
- 2 brazil nuts
- 1 scoop greens powder

Method

1. Place the spinach (or kale) in a high-speed blender.
2. Add in the almonds, brazil nuts and psyllium seeds into the blender
3. Pour the coconut milk and blend on high for 60 seconds until creamy and smooth
4. Add the greens powder and blend once again on high for 45 seconds until rich and creamy
5. Transfer into a glass and serve immediately.

Nutrition Information per Serving:

Calories 486 Kcal (Fat: 27 g | Protein: 40 g | Net carb: 3 g)

Low Carb Chocolate Almond Smoothie

Servings: 1

Ingredients

- 1 cup almond milk (unsweetened)
- 1 tablespoon cacao powder
- 1/4 cup ice
- 2 tablespoon almond butter (salted, preferred)
- 1 half of avocado
- Stevia, to taste (optional)

Method

1. Place the avocado in the high-speed blender.
2. Pour the almond milk and add the ice to it.
3. You can add stevia if you want it sweet else you can skip the step.
4. Blend the contents on high for 60 seconds until smooth
5. Add the almond butter and cacao powder to the mixture.
6. Blend again on high for 45 seconds until creamy and smooth
7. Transfer to a glass and serve chilled. Enjoy!

Nutrition Information per Serving:

Calories 208 Kcal (Fat: 39.2 g | Protein: 34.9 g | Net carb: 2.9 g)

Low Carb Strawberry Crunch Smoothie

Servings: 1

Ingredients

- 1/2 cup organic strawberries (frozen)
- 1 cup + 1 tablespoon vanilla almond milk (unsweetened)
- 2 tablespoons almonds
- 1 tablespoon chia seeds
- 1/2-teaspoon cinnamon.

Method

1. Place the frozen strawberries in the high-speed blender.
2. Pour one cup of almond milk into the blender.
3. Add the almonds and chia seeds to the contents.
4. Blend on high for 60 seconds or more until thick and creamy
5. Add the cinnamon and one tablespoon almond milk.
6. Blend once more on high for 45 seconds until smooth.
7. Transfer into a glass and serve immediately. Enjoy!

Nutrition Information per Serving:
Calories 332 Kcal (Fat: 31 g | Protein: 25 g | Net carb: 2 g)

Chocolate Coconut Keto Smoothie Bowl

Servings: 1

Ingredients

- 2 tablespoons raw cacao powder or cocoa powder (unsweetened)
- 3/4 cup full-fat coconut milk (organic)
- 1/4 cup ice
- 15-20 drops liquid coconut stevia
- 1 tablespoon grated coconut (unsweetened)

Method

1. Place the ice in the high-speed blender and pour the coconut milk into it.
2. Add the cocoa powder or cacao powder along with liquid coconut stevia.
3. Blend on high for 60 seconds until thick, creamy and smooth.
4. Transfer to a bowl and top it with grated coconut.
5. Serve chilled and enjoy!

Nutrition Information per Serving:
Calories 500 Kcal (Fat: 38 g | Protein: 26 g | Net carb: 4 g)

Chocolate Strawberry Smoothie Bowl

Servings: 2

Ingredients

- 4 tablespoons cacao powder or cocoa powder, unsweetened
- 1/4 cup chopped walnuts
- 1 1/2 cups almond milk (unsweetened)
- 4 scoops collagen protein
- 3 cups ice (crushed)
- Stevia drops to taste
- 2 large strawberries
- Stevia sweetened chocolate shavings to garnish
- Strawberry slices to garnish

Method

1. Add all the ingredients except collagen into a blender.
2. Blend on high for 50-60 seconds or until smooth.
3. Add collagen and pulse for 2-3 seconds until just combined.
4. Pour into bowls. Serve with chocolate shavings and strawberry slices.

Nutrition Information per Serving:
Calories 305 Kcal (Fat: 30 g | Protein: 35 g | Net carb: 2.1 g)

Keto Chia Smoothie Bowl

Servings: 1

Ingredients

- 2 tablespoons chia seeds
- 2 tablespoons desiccated coconut
- 14 fluid ounces coconut cream (unsweetened)
- 1/4 cup blueberries
- 1/2 avocado
- 1/4 cup water
- 1 teaspoon vanilla extract
- 1 teaspoon Erythritol (optional)

Method

1. Place the avocado in the high-speed blender and the coconut cream to it.
2. Pour water into the contents and blend on high for 60 seconds until smooth and thick
3. Add the vanilla extract and erythritol to the mixture.
4. Blend again on high for 45 seconds until smooth and creamy.
5. Transfer the smoothie to a bowl and top it with chia seeds, desiccated coconut and blueberries.
6. Serve immediately and enjoy!

Nutrition Information per Serving:

Calories 456 Kcal (Fat: 45 g | Protein: 6 g | Net carb: 3 g)

5 Minute Low Carb Smoothie Bowl

Servings: 1

Ingredients

- 1 cup spinach (washed and cleaned)
- 2 tablespoons heavy cream
- 1/2 cup almond milk
- 2 ice cubes
- 1 tablespoon melted coconut oil
- 1 tablespoon shredded coconut
- 4 raspberries
- 1 teaspoon chia seeds
- 4 walnuts (chopped)

Method

1. Place the spinach in the high-speed blender and pour the almond milk into it.
2. Add the ice cubes and blend on high for 60 seconds until smooth.
3. Add the heavy cream and blend again on high for 45 seconds.
4. Add the melted coconut oil as the blender continues to run.
5. Transfer the thick smoothie to a bowl.
6. Top it with shredded coconut, raspberries, chia seeds and chopped walnuts.
7. Serve chilled and enjoy!

Nutrition Information per Serving:

Calories 319 Kcal (Fat: 26 g | Protein: 10 g | Net carb: 5 g)

Keto Green Smoothie Bowl

Servings: 1

Ingredients

- 1 tablespoon MCT oil
- 1 cup kale (washed and cleaned)
- 3/4 cup coconut milk (unsweetened)
- 2 tablespoons lemon juice
- 1/2 medium avocado
- 1/4 cup ice cubes
- 1/4 cup Erythritol
- 1 teaspoon coconut flakes
- 1 tablespoon frozen strawberries
- 1/2 teaspoon Chia seeds
- 1 teaspoon Hemp seeds

Method

1. Place the kale in a high-speed blender and pour the coconut milk into it.
2. Add the avocado, ice cubes and erythritol to the contents.
3. Blend on high for 60 seconds until creamy and smooth
4. Add the lemon juice and MCT oil to the mixture.
5. Blend once again for 45 seconds until you get a thick creamy texture.
6. Transfer to a bowl and top it with coconut flakes, strawberries, chia seeds and hemp seeds.
7. Serve chilled and enjoy!

Nutrition Information per Serving:

Calories 320 Kcal (Fat: 30 g | Protein: 25 g | Net carb: 2.5 g)

Chapter Nine: Keto Breakfast recipes

Egg Vegetable Frittata

Servings: 6

Ingredients

- 10 ounces finely chopped spinach
- 5 eggs
- 1 cup chopped broccoli (pre-cooked)
- 3 cherry tomatoes halved
- 1/2 cup finely chopped fresh celery leaves
- 1/4 cup chopped red bell pepper
- 1/2 cup cheddar cheese
- 5 tablespoons olive oil
- 1/2 cup fresh ricotta cheese
- 1/4 teaspoon dried oregano
- 1/4 teaspoon freshly ground black pepper
- 1/2 teaspoon salt

Method

1. Preheat the oven to 400 degrees Fahrenheit
2. Grease a large skillet with olive oil and heat it up over medium-high heat
3. Add the spinach to the hot skillet and stir well. Reduce the heat to medium and cook for 5 minutes as you continue to stir.
4. Add the broccoli, tomatoes and bell pepper to the wilted spinach.
5. Add 2 tablespoons of olive oil and continue to stir. Let it cook for 4 minutes
6. Crack two eggs in a small bowl and add the ricotta and cheddar to it. Whisk together until well combined. Sprinkle the required salt and whisk again.
7. Add this to the veggies in the skillet and cook for another 2 minutes. Check for taste and add more salt if necessary.

8. Now crack the remaining three eggs directly into the skillet and remove from stovetop.
9. Place the skillet in the oven and bake for 5 minutes until the eggs are completely set.
10. Turn off the oven and sprinkle the celery leaves over the frittata. Drizzle over the remaining olive oil
11. Serve hot and enjoy!

Nutrition Information per Serving:
Calories 240 Kcal (Fat: 20 g | Protein: 11.3 g | Net carb: 3.5 g)

Three-cheese Pizza Frittata

Servings: 4

Ingredients

- 1/4 cup ricotta cheese
- 1-ounce pepperoni (sliced)
- 2 1/2 ounces mozzarella cheese (shredded)
- 6 eggs (large ones)
- 1/4 cup parmesan cheese (grated)
- 5 ounces frozen spinach, thawed
- 1/2 teaspoon Italian seasoning (dried)
- 2 tablespoons olive oil
- Salt and pepper, to taste
- Nonstick cooking spray

Method

1. Preheat oven to 375 degrees Fahrenheit
2. Use a cooking spray to grease the pie plate and keep aside.
3. Place the frozen spinach in the microwave and defrost for 5 minutes. Once done, squeeze out the water completely
4. Take a large bowl and crack the eggs into it.
5. Add the salt, pepper, olive oil and the Italian seasoning into the cracked eggs in the bowl.
6. Whisk the contents together until well combined.
7. Now, add the drained spinach, Parmesan cheese and ricotta cheese into the egg mixture.
8. Mix the contents thoroughly until they are incorporated well.
9. Pour this mixture into the greased pie plate and top it with pepperoni and mozzarella
10. Bake for 40 minutes until the cheese is slightly browned and the egg is perfectly set.

11. Remove from the oven and let it cool for some time.
12. Slice the pies and transfer to a plate. Serve hot and enjoy!

Nutrition Information per Serving:

Calories 301.13 Kcal (Fat: 13.48 g | Protein: 18.87 g | Net carb: 2.74 g)

Easy Cloud Buns

Servings: 10

Ingredients

- 3 ounces chopped cream cheese
- 8 teaspoons cream of tartar
- 3 eggs, separated (large ones)

Method

1. Preheat the oven to 300 degrees Fahrenheit
2. Line a baking tray with parchment and set aside
3. Place the egg whites in a large bowl and beat them until foamy.
4. Add in the cream of tartar to the beaten egg whites and whisk well until you see soft peaks and the whites look shiny
5. Take another medium-sized bowl and place the egg yolks in it.
6. Add the cream cheese to the egg yolks and beat them together until combined well.
7. Fold in the egg white mixture into the yolk mixture carefully.
8. Spoon this batter in 1/4-cup circle-format on the lined baking sheet.
9. Leave 2 inches gap between each circle and bake for 30 minutes until firm.
10. Remove from oven and let it cool.
11. Transfer to a plate and serve warm. Enjoy!

Nutrition Information per Serving:

Calories 76 Kcal (Fat: 6 g | Protein: 3 g | Net carb: 0 g)

Veggie Frittata

Servings: 2 to 3

Ingredients

- 2 cups baby spinach
- 1 chopped avocado
- 1 chopped tomato
- 1 minced garlic clove
- 1/4 diced onion
- 6 eggs
- 1/2 tablespoon nutritional yeast
- 3 tablespoons avocado oil (or coconut oil), divided
- 1/2 teaspoon ground cumin
- 2 tablespoons coconut milk
- 1/4 teaspoon chili powder
- Sea salt and black pepper, to taste

Method

1. Preheat oven to 350 degrees Fahrenheit.
2. Grease a small baking dish with a bit of coconut oil and set aside
3. Crack the eggs into a medium-sized bowl and add the salt, pepper, chili powder, coconut milk, ground cumin and nutritional yeast.
4. Whisk together the contents in the bowl until the mixture turns frothy
5. Heat the remaining coconut oil over medium-high heat in a skillet.
6. Add the onions and garlic to the hot oil.
7. Season with pepper and salt. Stir-fry until the contents turn fragrant as you continue to mix well.

8. Add the avocado to the onion-garlic mixture and sauté for 5 minutes.
9. Now, add the baby spinach and stir well until the spinach wilts
10. Transfer the sautéed vegetables to the greased baking dish and top it with the chopped tomato.
11. Pour the egg mixture over the tomato and mixed veggies until the contents are covered with the mixture
12. Bake for 25 minutes until the contents are cooked well and the eggs puff up.
13. Remove from the oven and let it cool
14. Transfer the veggie frittata to a plate and serve warm

Nutrition Information per Serving:

Calories 487 Kcal (Fat: 38 g | Protein: 26 g | Net carb: 4 g)

Mozzarella Veggie-loaded Quiche

Servings: 2

Ingredients

- 1/4 cup mozzarella cheese (shredded)
- 1 tablespoon parmesan cheese (grated)
- 4 cherry tomatoes, halved
- 1/4 cup spinach (frozen), thawed and well-drained
- 6 tablespoons almond flour
- 1/4 cup zucchini (diced)
- 2 large eggs, divided
- 1 teaspoon chives (chopped)
- 1 tablespoon heavy cream
- Salt and pepper, to taste
- Nonstick cooking spray

Method

1. Preheat the oven to 325 degrees Fahrenheit
2. Crack one egg into a large bowl and add the grated Parmesan, almond flour and a pinch of salt to it.
3. Mix well until the contents are well-blended and form a soft dough
4. Grease a small quiche pan with a cooking spray and transfer the egg-cheese-flour dough into the pan.
5. Press the dough well into the bottom of the pan and spread it evenly.
6. Score the sides and bottom of the dough. Bake for 7 minutes and let it cool
7. Add the tomatoes, zucchini and spinach to the baked dough. Sprinkle the mozzarella cheese over it and set aside.

8. Crack the remaining egg into a large bowl and add salt, pe heavy cream and chives into it.
9. Whisk the contents together completely and pour this mixtur into the set quiche
10. Bake for 25 minutes until cooked thoroughly and the egg is set.
11. Transfer to a plate and serve hot.

Nutrition Information per Serving:

Calories 215 Kcal (Fat: 16 g | Protein: 12 g | Net carb: 1.5 g)

- _ cups almond flour
- 6 tbsp psyllium husk powder (ground)
- 3 tsp baking powder
- 2 tsp sea salt
- 3 tsp cider vinegar
- 1 1/2 cups boiling water
- 4 egg whites

Garnish

- 3 tbsp sesame seeds (optional)

Sides

- 2 tbsp butter

Method

1. Preheat the oven to 300 degrees Fahrenheit.
2. Combine the dry ingredients in a large mixing bowl.
3. Add the boiling water, egg whites and vinegar to the bowl and beat the ingredients with a hand mixer for 30 seconds. Ensure that the consistency of the dough resembles Play-Doh.
4. Line a baking tray with parchment paper.
5. Moisten your hands and divide the dough into six pieces.
6. Place the six pieces on the prepared baking tray, and place the tray in the lower rack in the oven.

7. Bake for 60 minutes. When the timer goes off, tap the bun at the bottom. If you hear a hollow sound, they are done.
8. Serve warm with butter.

Nutrition Information per Serving:

Calories 109 Kcal (Fat: 5.5 g | Protein: 7.3 g | Net carb: 1.3 g)

BLT with cloud bread

Servings: 2
Ingredients

- 2 eggs
- 2 1/2 ounces cream cheese
- 1 tsp salt
- 1/4 tbsp psyllium husk powder (ground)
- 1/4 tsp baking powder
- 1/8 tsp cream of tartar

Toppings

- 2 tbsp mayonnaise
- 1 ounce bacon
- 1 ounce lettuce
- 1 tomato (sliced)
- 1 tbsp chopped basil (fresh)

Method
For the bread

1. Preheat the oven to 250 degrees Fahrenheit.
2. Crack the eggs and separate the egg whites from the yolk in different bowls.
3. Add salt and cream of tartar to the eggs whites and whip until you obtain a stiff mixture.
4. Add psyllium husk powder, baking powder and cream cheese to the yolks and whisk well.
5. Add the egg white mixture to the yolk mixture and whisk until the ingredients are well combined.
6. Line a bread tray with parchment paper and transfer the mixture into the tray.

7. Bake for 30 minutes or until the bread has turned golden.

For the BLT

1. Place a skillet over medium heat and fry the bacon until it is crispy.
2. Slice the bread and spread mayonnaise on each slice.
3. Place the lettuce, bacon, tomatoes and chopped basil in between the slices.
4. Serve immediately.

Nutrition Information per Serving:

Calories 498 Kcal (Fat: 48 g | Protein: 11 g | Net carb: 4 g)

Sweet Blueberry Coconut Porridge

Servings: 2

Ingredients

- 1/2 cup blueberries (fresh)
- 1/4 cup shredded coconut
- 1/4 cup coconut flour
- 1/4 cup coconut milk (canned)
- 1 cup almond milk (unsweetened)
- 1/4 teaspoon ground nutmeg
- 1/4 cup ground flaxseed
- Salt, to taste
- 1 teaspoon ground cinnamon
- Sweetener, to taste (optional)
- 1/4 teaspoon vanilla extract

Method

1. Pour the coconut milk and almond milk into a saucepan.
2. Warm the milk combo over low heat and add the cinnamon, salt, flaxseed, nutmeg and coconut flour into it.
3. Whisk it thoroughly until the mixture is well-combined (should be in low flame)
4. Increase the heat to high flame and continue to cook until the mixture begins to bubble
5. Add the vanilla extract and sweetener to the porridge. Mix well and let it cook until the mixture thickens.
6. Transfer the porridge to serving bowls and top it with shredded coconut and blueberries.
7. Serve warm and enjoy!

Nutrition Information per Serving:

Calories 405 Kcal (Fat: 34 g | Protein: 10 g | Net carb: 3 g)

Avocado and Salmon Low-Carb Breakfast

Servings: 1

Ingredients

- 1 deseeded ripe avocado (organic)
- 1 ounce soft goat cheese (fresh)
- 2 ounces smoked salmon (wild caught)
- Juice of 1 lemon
- 2 tablespoons extra virgin olive oil (organic)
- Sea salt, to taste

Method

1. Chop the avocado into small cubes and salmon into small pieces
2. Mix the cubed avocado and salmon pieces in a small bowl
3. Add the goat cheese, olive oil, salt and the lemon juice to the contents in the bowl.
4. Mix the contents thoroughly and transfer it to a high-speed blender.
5. Blend the mixture coarsely and serve immediately. Enjoy!

Nutrition Information per Serving:

Calories 525 Kcal (Fat: 48 g | Protein: 19 g | Net carb: 4 g)

Eggs and Steak

Servings: 1

Ingredients

- 3 eggs
- 4 ounces sirloin
- 2 tablespoons butter
- 1/4 avocado (sliced into cubes)
- Salt and pepper, to taste

Method

1. Melt one tablespoon butter in a saucepan over low heat and crack in the eggs into it
2. Fry the eggs until the yolk gets cooked thoroughly and the whites are set
3. Add the required salt and pepper. Mix the contents thoroughly.
4. Heat another pan and cook the sirloin in the remaining butter until the meat is soft and tender.
5. Using the spatula, break the meat into small pieces. Season with salt and pepper, and mix the contents thoroughly.
6. Remove both the pans from heat and mix the contents together in a large bowl.
7. Transfer to a plate and serve with sliced avocado. Enjoy!

Nutrition Information per Serving:

Calories 692 Kcal (Fat: 51 g | Protein: 45 g | Net carb: 2.9 g)

Keto Zucchini Breakfast

Servings: 1

Ingredients

- 1 zucchini (medium-sized one), diced
- 1/2 avocado
- 1/2 cup mushrooms (cleaned and chopped)
- 1 tablespoon chives or parsley (freshly chopped)
- 1/2 white onion (small one), finely chopped
- 1 garlic clove (minced)
- 1/4 teaspoon salt
- 1 tablespoon coconut oil

Method

1. Heat the coconut oil in a pan over medium heat.
2. Add the chopped onion to the hot oil and sauté until translucent and completely off-liquid
3. Add the minced garlic and mix well until the raw flavor goes off
4. Add the chopped mushroom and sauté until the mushrooms are tender and cooked thoroughly
5. Continue to stir the contents until they turn slightly brown
6. Now, add the diced zucchini to the pan and continue to cook for another 15 minutes until the entire contents are thoroughly cooked.
7. Season with salt and mix once more. Remove from heat and top it with parsley and avocado.
8. Transfer to a plate and serve warm. Enjoy!

Nutrition Information per Serving:

Calories 423 Kcal (Fat: 35.5 g | Protein: 17.4 g | Net carb: 3.6 g)

Poached Eggs with Spinach

Servings: 2

Ingredients

- 2 eggs
- 7 ounces chopped spinach
- 1/2 teaspoon garlic powder
- 3 tablespoons olive oil
- 1/4 teaspoon dried rosemary
- 1/4 teaspoon dried oregano
- 1/2 teaspoon sea salt

Method

1. Heat the oil in a saucepan over medium-high heat.
2. Add the chopped spinach to the hot oil and sauté for 5 minutes
3. Add garlic powder and a pinch of salt to the spinach as you continue to stir the contents.
4. Crack the eggs into the pan gently and mix well.
5. Add the remaining salt, oregano and rosemary to the egg and spinach. Mix well and let it cook for 5 more minutes until the egg sets.
6. Remove from heat and transfer to a plate. Serve warm and enjoy!

Nutrition Information per Serving:

Calories 269 Kcal (Fat: 25.2 g | Protein: 8.5 g | Net carb: 2.3 g)

Keto Pancake

Servings: 4 pancakes

Ingredients

- 3 eggs
- 1 tablespoon almond flour
- 2 ounces cream cheese
- 1 teaspoon garlic powder
- 1/4 teaspoon powdered stevia
- 5 tablespoons coconut oil
- 1/4 teaspoon black pepper (freshly ground)
- 1 teaspoon salt

Method

1. Crack the eggs into a mixing bowl and add the cream cheese to it.
2. Whisk the eggs and cheese together thoroughly.
3. Add the salt, pepper and garlic powder to the egg-cheese mixture
4. Add the stevia and almond flour to the mixture. Beat the contents on high speed for three minutes and set the batter aside
5. Heat a large pan over medium heat and add a bit coconut oil (to grease the skillet)
6. Pour two tablespoons of the mixed batter into the hot skillet.
7. Allow it to cook for 2 minutes until completely set.
8. Using a spatula, flip the pancake to the other side and cook for one minute
9. Repeat steps 6 to 8 with the remaining batter.
10. Transfer to a plate and serve hot. Enjoy!

Nutrition Information per Serving:

Calories 580 Kcal (Fat: 50 g | Protein: 25 g | Net carb: 6 g)

Swiss chard and Spinach Omelet

Servings: 3

Ingredients

- 7 ounces Swiss chard (washed, drained and chopped)
- 7 ounces fresh spinach (washed, drained and chopped)
- 3 eggs
- 1/4 teaspoon chili flakes
- 1 tablespoon butter
- 3 tablespoons coconut oil
- 1 teaspoon sea salt
- 1 teaspoon Italian seasoning mix

Method

1. Heat the coconut oil over medium-high heat in a large skillet.
2. Add the chopped greens (both spinach and Swiss chard) to the hot oil and mix well.
3. Cook for 10 minutes as you continue to stir once in a while and add the required salt.
4. Remove from heat and set aside.
5. Crack the eggs into a small bowl and beat them well until combined
6. Melt the butter in another saucepan and pour the beaten eggs into the hot pan
7. Season with chili flakes, Italian seasoning and the remaining salt.
8. Let it cook for 4 minutes until the egg is completely set
9. Transfer the omelet to a serving plate and add the cooked greens over it.
10. Fold the omelet and serve warm. Enjoy!

Nutrition Information per Serving:

Calories 245 Kcal (Fat: 22.3 g | Protein: 8.7 g | Net carb: 2.6 g)

Cheesy Cauliflower

Servings: 4

Ingredients

- 1 small head cauliflower (chopped into small florets)
- 1 1/2 cup mozzarella cheese
- 2 eggs
- 2 minced garlic cloves
- 1 tablespoon butter
- 1 tablespoon almond flour
- 1 teaspoon rosemary
- Salt and pepper, to taste
- 1 teaspoon oregano

Method

1. Pulse the cauliflower florets in a food processor until you get a grainy rice texture
2. Transfer the cauliflower rice grains to a heat-safe bowl and add a tablespoon of butter to it.
3. Mix them together and place the bowl in the microwave. Set to the cooking mode and cook for 1 minute and 30 seconds
4. Transfer the cooked cauliflower into a large bowl and crack the eggs into it.
5. Add oregano, salt, pepper, rosemary, almond flour, minced garlic and one cup of mozzarella into the bowl.
6. Mix together the contents thoroughly until the flavors are well incorporated and set aside.
7. Preheat the oven to 300 degrees Fahrenheit
8. Line a baking tray with parchment paper and transfer the mixture to the tray.

9. Spread the mixture evenly and pat on all sides. Top it with remaining mozzarella cheese until the surface is covered.
10. Bake for 15 minutes until the contents are set and cheese turns golden.
11. Let it stand for 5 minutes and allow it to cool.
12. Slice the cheesy cauliflower and transfer to a plate. Serve warm and enjoy!

Nutrition Information per Serving:

Calories 366 Kcal (Fat: 29 g | Protein: 16 g | Net carb: 3 g)

Keto Deviled Eggs

Servings: 2

Ingredients

- 4 medium eggs
- 3 tablespoons low carb Mayonnaise
- 1 teaspoon Dijon mustard
- 1/4 teaspoon cayenne pepper
- 1/4 teaspoon paprika
- Salt and ground black pepper, to taste

Method

1. Hard boil all the four eggs for 7 minutes and drain the water and peel the shells off.
2. Slice them lengthwise into two halves.
3. Scoop the yolks for the egg and place the yolks separately in a small bowl.
4. Add the mayonnaise, Dijon mustard, cayenne pepper and salt to the yolks. Mash them well and mix until the flavors are blended.
5. Spoon the spiced yolks into the egg whites and garnish with paprika and black pepper.
6. Transfer to a plate and serve immediately. Enjoy!

Nutrition Information per Serving:

Calories 264 Kcal (Fat: 23.9 g | Protein: 11.3 g | Net carb: 0.9 g)

Chapter Ten: Fish and Chicken Keto Recipes

Keto fish and chips

Servings: 4

Course: Lunch

Ingredients

For the Tartar Sauce

- 4 tablespoons dill pickle relish
- 1 cup mayonnaise
- 1/2 tablespoon curry powder

For the chips

- 1 tablespoon olive oil
- 1 1/2 pounds rutabaga (peeled and cleaned)
- Salt and pepper, to taste

For the fish

- 1 1/2 pounds white fish
- 1 cup parmesan cheese (grated)
- 1 cup almond flour
- 2 eggs
- 2 cups coconut oil, for frying
- 1 teaspoon paprika powder
- 1/4 teaspoon pepper
- 1/2 teaspoon onion powder
- 1 lemon
- 1 teaspoon salt

Method

1. Take a small bowl and mix together mayonnaise, curry powder and pickle relish thoroughly. Refrigerate the tartar sauce until you finish the remaining dish.
2. Preheat the oven to 400 degrees Fahrenheit.
3. Slice the peeled rutabaga into thin rods and brush them with oil.
4. Line a baking tray with parchment paper and spread the oil-coated rutabaga rods.
5. Sprinkle the pepper and salt over the spread rutabaga.
6. Bake for 30 minutes until the rods become golden brown.
7. As the rutabaga gets cooked, prepare the fish.
8. Crack the eggs into a small bowl and beat it well with a fork.
9. Mix the Parmesan cheese, almond flour, paprika powder, pepper, onion powder and salt in a plate. Set aside.
10. Slice the fish into small bite-sized pieces and coat it with the flour mix.
11. Dip the flour-coated fix into the beaten eggs and coat it again with the flour mix.
12. Pour the oil in a shallow skillet and heat over high heat.
13. If the rutabaga chips are ready by now, turn off the oven and let it sit for a while.
14. Fry the flour-egg coated fish in the hot oil until the fish is completely cooked and turns golden brown.
15. Repeat the step 11 and 14 with the remaining fish.
16. Transfer the fried fish, baked rutabaga fries and tartar into a serving bowl.
17. Serve hot and enjoy!

Nutrition Information per Serving:
Calories 463 Kcal (Fat: 26.2 g | Protein: 49.2 g | Net carb: 4 g)

Zingy Lemon Fish

Servings: 4

Ingredients:

- 14 ounces fresh Gurnard fish fillets
- 2 tablespoons lemon juice
- 6 tablespoons butter
- ½ cup fine almond flour
- 2 teaspoons dried chives
- 1 teaspoon garlic powder
- 2 teaspoons dried dill
- 2 teaspoons onion powder
- Salt and pepper to taste

Method:

1. Add almond flour, dried herbs, salt and spices on a large plate and stir until well combined. Spread it all over the plate evenly.
2. Dredge the fish fillets in the almond flour mixture, all over and place on another plate.
3. Place a large pan over medium-high heat. Add half the butter and half the lemon juice. When butter just melts, place fillets on the pan and cook for 3 minutes. Move the fillets around the pan so that it absorbs the butter and lemon juice.

4. Add remaining half butter and lemon juice. When butter melts, flip sides and cook the other side for 3 minutes.

5. Move the fillets around the pan again so that it absorbs the butter and lemon juice. When the fish is cooked, it will flake easily when pierced with a fork.

6. Serve fillets with any butter remaining in the pan.

Nutrition Information per Serving:
Calories 406 Kcal (Fat: 30.33 g | Protein: 29 g | Net carb: 3.55 g)

Creamy keto fish casserole

Servings: 4

Course: Dinner

Ingredients

- 25 ounces of white fish (slice into bite-sized pieces)
- 15 ounces broccoli (small florets, include the step too)
- 3 ounces butter + extra
- 6 scallions (finely chopped)
- 1 1/4 cups heavy whipping cream
- 2 tablespoons small capers
- 1 tablespoon dried parsley
- 1 tablespoon Dijon mustard
- 1/4 teaspoon black pepper (ground)
- 1 teaspoon salt
- 2 tablespoons olive oil
- 5 ounces leafy greens (finely chopped), for garnishing

Method

1. Preheat the oven to 400 degrees Fahrenheit
2. Heat the oil in a saucepan over medium-high heat.
3. Fry the broccoli florets in the hot oil for 5 minutes until tender and golden.
4. Transfer the fried florets to a small bowl and season it with salt and pepper. Toss the contents to ensure all the florets get the equal amount of seasoning.
5. Add the chopped scallions and capers to the same saucepan and fry for 2 minutes. Return the florets to the pan and mix well.
6. Grease a baking tray with a little amount of butter and spread the fried veggies (broccoli, scallions, and capers) in the baking tray.
7. Add the sliced fish to the tray and nestle it among the veggies.
8. Mix the heavy cream, mustard and parsley in a small bowl and pour this mixture over the fish-veggie mixture
9. Top this with the remaining butter and spread gently over the contents using a spatula
10. Bake for 20 minutes until the fish is cooked thoroughly and the cream and butter melt lusciously.
11. Transfer to a plate and garnish with chopped greens. Serve warm and enjoy!

Nutrition Information per Serving:

Calories 822 Kcal (Fat: 69 g | Protein: 41 g | Net carb: 8 g)

Keto fish casserole with mushrooms and French mustard

Servings: 6

Course: Lunch or Dinner

Ingredients

- 25 ounces of white fish
- 15 ounces mushrooms (cut into wedges)
- 20 ounces cauliflower (cut into florets)
- 2 cups heavy whipping cream
- 3 ounces butter
- 2 tablespoons Dijon mustard
- 3 ounces olive oil
- 8 ounces cheese (shredded)
- 2 tablespoons fresh parsley
- Salt & pepper, to taste

Method

1. Preheat the oven to 350 degrees Fahrenheit
2. Melt the butter in a skillet over medium heat and add the mushroom wedges to it.
3. Fry the mushroom for 5 minutes until tender and soft.
4. Add the parsley, salt and pepper to the mushrooms as you continue to mix well.
5. Reduce the heat and add the mustard and heavy whipping cream to the mushroom.
6. Allow it simmer for 10 minutes until the sauce thickens and reduces a bit.
7. Season the fish slices with pepper and salt. Set aside.

8. Grease a baking tray with a bit of olive oil and place the fish slices in it.
9. Sprinkle 3/4th of the cheese over the fish slices and spread the creamy mushroom over the top. Now again top it with the remaining cheese.
10. Bake for 30 minutes until the fish is cooked well such that it flakes easily. Turn off the oven and let it sit.
11. Boil the cauliflower florets in lightly salted water for 5 minutes and strain the water.
12. Place the strained florets in a bowl and add the olive oil. Mash thoroughly with a fork until you get a coarse texture. Season with salt and pepper. Mix well.
13. Transfer the cooked fish to a plate and serve with the mashed cauliflower. Enjoy!

Nutrition Information per Serving:

Calories 828 Kcal (Fat: 71 g | Protein: 39 g | Net carb: 8 g)

Keto Thai fish with curry and coconut

Servings: 4

Course: Lunch

Ingredients

- 25 ounces salmon (slice into bite-sized pieces)
- 15 ounces cauliflower (bite-sized florets)
- 14 ounces coconut cream
- 1 ounce olive oil
- 2 tablespoons green curry paste or red curry paste
- 1/2 cup chopped fresh cilantro
- 4 tablespoons butter
- Salt and pepper, to taste

Method

1. Preheat the oven to 400 degrees Fahrenheit
2. Grease a baking tray with olive oil and place the salmon pieces on the tray.
3. Sprinkle salt and pepper over the salmon generously. Toss it once if possible.
4. Place the butter generously over all the salmon pieces and set aside.
5. Take a small bowl and place the cilantro in it. Add the coconut cream and curry paste to the cilantro. Mix thoroughly until the flavors are well blended.
6. Pour this cream mixture over the fish in the baking tray.
7. Bake for 20 minutes until the fish is thoroughly cooked.
8. Meanwhile, boil the cauliflower florets in salted water for 5 minutes, strain and mash the florets coarsely. Set aside.
9. Transfer the creamy fish to a plate and serve with mashed cauliflower. Enjoy!

Nutrition Information per Serving:

Calories 880 Kcal (Fat: 75 g | Protein: 42 g | Net carb: 6 g)

Keto salmon Tandoori with cucumber sauce

Servings: 4

Course: Dinner

Ingredients

- 25 ounces salmon (bite-sized pieces)
- 2 tablespoons coconut oil
- 1 tablespoon tandoori seasoning

For the cucumber sauce
- 1/2 shredded cucumber (squeeze out the water completely)
- Juice of 1/2 lime
- 2 minced garlic cloves
- 1 1/4 cups sour cream or mayonnaise
- 1/2 teaspoon salt (optional)

For the crispy salad
- 3 1/2 ounces lettuce (torn)
- 3 scallions (finely chopped)
- 2 avocados (cubed)
- 1 yellow bell pepper (diced)
- Juice of 1 lime

Method

1. Preheat the oven to 350 degrees Fahrenheit
2. Mix the tandoori seasoning with oil in a small bowl and coat the salmon pieces with this mixture.
3. Line the baking tray with parchment paper and spread the coated salmon pieces in it.
4. Bake for 20 minutes until soft and the salmon flakes with a fork

5. Take another bowl and place the shredded cucumber in it. Add the mayonnaise, minced garlic and salt (if the mayonnaise doesn't have salt) to the shredded cucumber. Mix well. Squeeze the lime juice over the top and set the cucumber sauce aside.
6. Mix the lettuce, scallions, avocados and bell pepper in another bowl. Drizzle the contents with the lime juice.
7. Transfer the veggie salad to a plate and place the baked salmon over it. Top the veggies and salmon with cucumber sauce.
8. Serve immediately and enjoy!

Nutrition Information per Serving:
Calories 847 Kcal (Fat: 73 g | Protein: 35 g | Net carb: 6 g)

Low-carb garlic chicken

Servings: 4

Course: Dinner

Ingredients

- 2 pounds chicken drumsticks
- 10 minced garlic cloves
- 1/2 cup finely chopped fresh parsley
- 2 tablespoons olive oil
- 4 tablespoons butter
- Juice of 1 lemon

Method

1. Preheat the oven to 450 degrees Fahrenheit
2. Grease the baking tray with 1-tablespoon butter.
3. Place the chicken in the greased baking tray and sprinkle generously with pepper and salt.
4. Now, sprinkle the parsley and garlic over the chicken. Drizzle with the olive oil and lemon juice on the top finally.
5. Bake for 40 minutes until the chicken is roasted and minced garlic turns brown.
6. Reduce the temperature towards the last 10 minutes and let it cook.
7. Transfer the garlic chicken to the plate. Serve warm and enjoy!

Nutrition Information per Serving:

Calories 546 Kcal (Fat: 39 g | Protein: 42 g | Net carb: 3 g)

Keto chicken and cabbage plate

Servings: 2

Course: Dinner

Ingredients

- 1 pound rotisserie chicken
- 1/2 red onion (finely sliced)
- 7 ounces shredded green cabbage (fresh)
- 1/2 cup mayonnaise
- 1 tablespoon olive oil
- Salt and pepper, to taste

Method

1. Place the rotisserie chicken in a large plate and add the shredded cabbage to it.
2. Add the onion to the chicken-cabbage mixture and generously top it with mayonnaise.
3. Drizzle with the olive oil over the mixture and season with salt and pepper.
4. Mix well and serve immediately. Enjoy!

Nutrition Information per Serving:

Calories 1041 Kcal (Fat: 91 g | Protein: 48 g | Net carb: 5 g)

Keto chicken wings with creamy broccoli

Servings: 4

Course: Dinner

Ingredients

For the baked chicken wings

- 3 pounds chicken wings
- 1/4 teaspoon cayenne pepper
- 1/2 orange, zest and juice
- 2 teaspoons ground ginger
- 1/4 cup olive oil + extra
- 1 teaspoon salt

For the creamy broccoli

- 25 pounds broccoli (chopped into small florets)
- 1/4 cup fresh dill (chopped)
- 1 cup mayonnaise
- Salt and pepper, to taste

Method

1. Preheat the oven to 400 degrees Fahrenheit.
2. Take a small bowl and place the orange zest in it. Add the cayenne pepper, ground ginger and salt to the zest. Pour the orange juice and the oil to the contents. Mix thoroughly and set aside.
3. Place the chicken wings in a plastic zip bag and pour the prepared orange zest marinade into the plastic bag.
4. Shake the bag until the marinade mixes well with the chicken. Refrigerate the marinated chicken for 15 to 20 minutes.
5. Grease a baking tray with extra olive oil and place the marinated chicken wings in a single layer.

6. Bake for 45 minutes in the middle rack of the oven until the chicken is thoroughly cooked and browned.
7. Meanwhile, boil the broccoli florets in salted water for 10 minutes until they soften a bit.
8. Strain the boiled broccoli and transfer it to a bowl. Add the mayonnaise, dill, salt and pepper to the bowl. Mix well and set aside.
9. Transfer the cooked chicken to a serving plate and add the creamy broccoli over it. Serve warm and enjoy!

Nutrition Information per Serving:
Calories 1218 Kcal (Fat: 100 g | Protein: 65 g | Net carb: 3 g)

Oven-baked paprika chicken with rutabaga

Servings: 4

Course: Dinner

Ingredients

- 30 ounces chicken thighs
- 4 ounces butter
- 30 ounces rutabaga (peeled and diced)
- 1 cup mayonnaise
- 1 tablespoon paprika powder
- Salt and pepper, to taste

Method

1. Preheat the oven to 400 degrees Fahrenheit
2. Line the baking tray with baking paper and set aside
3. Place the diced rutabaga in a large bowl and add the chicken to it. Season with salt and pepper. Mix thoroughly until the flavors are incorporated.
4. Sprinkle paprika over the rutabaga-chicken mixture and add the butter to it. Toss the mixture well.
5. Spread the butter coated rutabaga-chicken mixture in the baking tray and let it bake for 40 minutes until thoroughly cooked
6. Lower the temperature as the contents turn golden brown
7. Transfer the cooked chicken to a plate and serve with mayonnaise. Enjoy!

Nutrition Information per Serving:

Calories 1165 Kcal (Fat: 103 g | Protein: 40 g | Net carb: 15 g)

Keto chicken casserole

Servings: 6

Course: Lunch

Ingredients

- 30 ounces chicken thighs
- 1 pound cauliflower (chopped into florets)
- 7 ounces shredded cheese
- 1 leek (coarsely chopped)
- 1 cup sour cream or heavy whipping cream
- 4 ounces cherry tomatoes (quartered)
- 2 tablespoons green pesto
- 3 tablespoons butter
- Juice of 1/2 lemon
- Salt and pepper, to taste

Method

1. Preheat the oven to 400 degrees Fahrenheit
2. Mix together the green pesto, lemon juice and heavy whipping cream in a small bowl.
3. Season with salt and pepper, and mix well. Set aside.
4. Take another small bowl and mix together desired amount of salt and pepper to season the chicken pieces. Season the chicken with the salt-pepper mixture.
5. Melt the butter in a large skillet over high heat and fry the seasoned chicken pieces until golden brown
6. Grease a baking tray with a bit of butter and place the fried butter chicken in it
7. Pour the pesto-cream mixture over the fried chicken in the tray and top it with cauliflower, leek and tomatoes.

8. Sprinkle the shredded cheese over the veggies and chicken cream mixture. Cover the baking tray with aluminum foil.
9. Bake for 30 minutes in the middle of the oven until the chicken is completely cooked.
10. Lower the heat toward the end and cook for 5 more minutes.
11. Transfer to a plate and serve hot. Enjoy!

Nutrition Information per Serving:

Calories 739 Kcal (Fat: 62 g | Protein: 37 g | Net carb: 4 g)

Keto chicken Garam masala

Servings: 4

Course: Lunch

Ingredients

- 25 ounces chicken breasts
- 1 finely diced red bell pepper
- 3 tablespoons butter
- 1 1/4 cups coconut cream
- 1 tablespoon finely chopped fresh parsley
- Salt, to taste

For the garam masala

- 1 teaspoon ground cumin
- 1 pinch ground nutmeg
- 1 teaspoon ground turmeric
- 2 teaspoons ground coriander seeds
- 1 teaspoon ground ginger
- 1 teaspoon chili powder
- 1 teaspoon ground green cardamom
- 1 teaspoon paprika powder

Method

1. Preheat the oven to 400 degrees Fahrenheit
2. Take a small bowl and mix together the paprika powder, ground cardamom, chili powder, ground ginger, coriander seeds, turmeric nutmeg and cumin thoroughly. Set the spice mixture aside.
3. Slice the chicken lengthwise and keep ready.

4. Heat the butter in a large pan over medium heat and add the chopped chicken to the melted butter.
5. Fry the chicken pieces until cooked and turns golden brown
6. Now add half of the spice mixture to the skillet and stir thoroughly until the garam masala gets coated over the fried chicken. Season with salt as per your desired taste and turn off the heat
7. Transfer the entire contents of the skillet (chicken and the saucy mixture) to a baking tray and set aside.
8. Take another small bowl and place the diced bell pepper in it. Add the coconut cream and the remaining spice mixture to it. Mix thoroughly.
9. Pour this creamy pepper mixture over the chicken in the baking tray and bake for 20 minutes.
10. Once done, transfer to a plate and garnish with parsley and serve hot! Enjoy!

Nutrition Information per Serving:

Calories 628 Kcal (Fat: 51 g | Protein: 38 g | Net carb: 6 g)

Chapter Eleven: Vegetarian Keto Recipes

Keto white pizza with mushrooms and pesto

Servings: 2

Course: Lunch

Ingredients

For the crust

- 2 eggs
- 3/4 cup almond flour
- 1 teaspoon baking powder
- 1 tablespoon psyllium husk powder
- 1/2 cup mayonnaise
- 1/2 teaspoon salt

For the topping

- 2 ounces mushrooms (finely sliced)
- 1/2 cup sour cream
- 1 tablespoon green pesto
- 3/4 cup shredded cheese
- 2 tablespoon olive oil
- Salt and pepper, to taste

Method

1. Preheat the oven to 350 degrees Fahrenheit
2. Crack the eggs into a large bowl and add mayonnaise to it.
3. Whisk together until you get a frothy and creamy mixture
4. Add the almond flour, baking powder, psyllium husk powder and salt to the egg-mayonnaise mixture
5. Mix thoroughly until the contents are blended well and let it sit for 5 minutes.
6. Line a baking tray with parchment and transfer the crust mixture into it.

7. Use a spatula to spread out the mixture evenly to prepare the crust (should be around 1/2 inch thick)
8. Bake for 10 minutes until the crust turns light golden brown – don't overdo and burn it.
9. Remove the crust from the oven and let it cool for 10 minutes.
10. Once cooled, turn out the crust into a cutting board and slowly remove the parchment paper
11. Place the sliced mushrooms into a small bowl and add the pesto into it.
12. Mix them well as you slowly add the olive oil too. Season with pepper and salt.
13. Combine the contents thoroughly until the flavors blend well
14. Layer out the sour cream on the prepared crust and top it with the shredded cheese
15. Now add the mushroom mixture and spread it out evenly
16. Use the same parchment paper to line the baking tray and place the pizza onto it
17. Return the pizza back to the oven and let it back for 10 minutes until the cheese melts.
18. Turn off the heat and slice out the pizza. Transfer to a plate and serve warm. Enjoy!

Nutrition Information per Serving:

Calories 1147 Kcal (Fat: 110 g | Protein: 27 g | Net carb: 7 g)

Keto grilled veggie plate

Servings: 2

Course: Dinner

Ingredients

- 1/2 eggplant
- 1 ounce leafy greens
- 1/2 zucchini
- 10 black olives
- 1/4 cup olive oil
- 1/2 cup mayonnaise
- 2 tablespoon almonds
- 7 ounces cheddar cheese
- Juice of 1/2 lemon
- Salt and pepper, to taste

Method

1. Slice the zucchini and the eggplant lengthwise to make thick slices (1/2 inch).
2. Rub the slices with salt on both sides and allow them to sit for 10 minutes
3. Preheat the oven to 450 degrees Fahrenheit or set it to broil (you can choose whichever you like)
4. Pat the zucchini and eggplant dry with paper towels until the surface is completely dry.
5. Line the baking tray with parchment paper and place the slices on it.
6. Brush the visible side with olive oil and sprinkle them with pepper
7. Bake or broil for 20 minutes and then flip to the other side halfway through until golden brown on both the sides.

8. Turn off the oven and transfer the broiled or baked veggies into a plate.
9. Top them with lemon juice, leafy greens, cheese and drizzle the olive oil.
10. Serve with olives and mayonnaise. Enjoy!

Nutrition Information per Serving:

Calories 1013 Kcal (Fat: 99 g | Protein: 21 g | Net carb: 9 g)

Keto Spinach and Goat Cheese Pie

Servings: 12

Ingredients:

For pie crust:

- 2 ½ cups almond flour
- 2 tablespoons psyllium husk powder
- 3 ounces butter
- 6 2/3 tablespoons sesame seeds
- 1 teaspoon salt
- 2 eggs

For egg batter:

- 10 eggs
- Salt and pepper to taste
- 2 cups heavy whipping cream or sour cream

For spinach and goat cheese filling:

- 14 ounces fresh spinach, coarsely chopped
- 2 cloves garlic, minced
- Salt and pepper to taste
- 12 ounces goat's cheese, sliced
- 4 tablespoons butter or coconut oil
- ¼ teaspoon ground nutmeg
- 7 ounces shredded cheese

Method:

1. Preheat the oven to 350 degrees Fahrenheit.

2. Add all the ingredients of piecrust into the food processor bowl and process until dough is formed.
3. Divide the dough into 2 equal portions. Spread in 2 spring form pans. Press it well onto the bottom of the pan.
4. Bake for 10 to 15 minutes.
5. To make egg batter: Add eggs into a bowl and whisk well. Add whipping cream, salt and pepper and whisk until well combined.
6. Add cheese and stir.
7. To make filling: Place a skillet over medium heat. Add butter. When butter melts, add garlic and cook until aromatic. Add the spinach and cook until the spinach wilts. Season as per requirement
8. Divide the spinach into the baked piecrusts. Pour egg batter over the spinach layer.
9. Sprinkle goat cheese on top.
10. Bake for 30 to 40 minutes or until the pie sets in the center.

Nutrition Information per Serving:

Calories 643 Kcal (Fat: 58 g | Protein: 24 g | Net carb: 4 g)

Keto avocado pie

Servings: 4

Course: Lunch

Ingredients

For the pie crust

- 3/4 cup almond flour
- 1 egg
- 4 tablespoons coconut flour
- 4 tablespoons sesame seeds
- 1 teaspoon baking powder
- 1 tablespoon ground psyllium husk powder
- 3 tablespoons olive oil or coconut oil
- 4 tablespoons water
- 1 pinch salt

For the filling

- 2 ripe avocados (peeled, deseeded and diced)
- 3 eggs
- 1 1/4 cups shredded cheese
- 1 cup mayonnaise
- 1/2 teaspoon onion powder
- 2 tablespoons finely chopped fresh cilantro
- 1/2 cup cream cheese
- 1 finely chopped red chili pepper (remove the seeds)
- 1/4 tsp salt

Method

1. Preheat the oven to 350 degrees Fahrenheit
2. Crack one egg into a large bowl and add a pinch of salt to it.
3. Now, add the psyllium husk powder, baking powder, sesame seeds, coconut flour and almond flour to the egg.
4. Mix thoroughly and once you get the dough texture, add the oil and water into the mixture.
5. Knead the dough together using your hands and set aside.
6. Line a parchment paper to a 12-inch springform pan and grease both the pan and paper with a bit of olive oil
7. Transfer the dough to the greased pan and spread it evenly using your oiled fingers or spatula.
8. Prebake the crust for 15 minutes.
9. Place the diced avocado and finely chopped chili in a bowl. Crack the eggs into it and add salt.
10. Now, add the cream cheese, mayonnaise and onion powder into the bowl. Mix the contents thoroughly until well combined.
11. Pour this mixture into the pre-baked piecrust and bake it for 35 minutes until it becomes golden brown.
12. Towards the end of the baking time, sprinkle the cilantro and shredded cheese generously over each pie.
13. Continue to bake until the cheese melts and turn off the oven.
14. Let it cool for 5 minutes and transfer to a plate. Serve warm and enjoy.

Nutrition Information per Serving:

Calories 1146 Kcal (Fat: 109 g | Protein: 26 g | Net carb: 9 g)

Keto mushroom and cheese frittata

Servings: 4

Course: Lunch

Ingredients

For the frittata

- 15 ounces mushrooms (chopped)
- 10 eggs
- 6 finely chopped scallions
- 4 ounces leafy greens
- 8 ounces shredded cheese
- 3 ounces butter + extra (for greasing)
- 1 cup mayonnaise
- 1 tablespoon fresh parsley
- 1/2 teaspoon ground black pepper
- 1 teaspoon salt

For the vinaigrette

- 1 tablespoon white wine vinegar
- 1/4 teaspoon ground black pepper
- 1/2 teaspoon salt
- 4 tablespoons olive oil

Method

1. Preheat the oven to 350 degrees Fahrenheit
2. Take a small bowl and mix together the white wine vinegar, black pepper, salt and olive oil thoroughly in it. Set the prepared vinaigrette aside.

3. Heat the butter in a skillet on medium-high heat and add the mushrooms to the hot melted butter
4. Sauté until the mushrooms turn golden and lower the heat.
5. Add the scallions to the fried mushroom and mix well. Season with salt and pepper as you continue to sauté the contents in the skillet.
6. Add the parsley and let it cook for few more seconds. Turn off the heat.
7. Crack the eggs into a separate bowl and add the cheese and mayonnaise into it.
8. Mix the egg-cheese-mayonnaise mixture well and season it with pepper and salt.
9. Add the prepared mushroom-scallion mixture to the egg mixture and combine well until the flavors are incorporated.
10. Grease a baking tray with butter and pour this egg-mushroom mixture into the greased tray.
11. Bake for 40 minutes until the eggs are thoroughly cooked and the frittata turns golden.
12. Remove from the oven and let it cool for 5 minutes.
13. Transfer the frittata onto a plate and sprinkle the leafy greens over it. Drizzle the vinaigrette and serve warm. Enjoy!

Nutrition Information per Serving:

Calories 1061 Kcal (Fat: 101 g | Protein: 32 g | Net carb: 6 g)

Keto mushroom omelet

Servings: 1

Course: Breakfast, Lunch or dinner

Ingredients

- 3 eggs
- 3 mushrooms (finely chopped)
- 1/2 yellow onion (finely chopped)
- 1 ounce butter
- Salt and pepper, to taste
- 1 ounce shredded cheese

Method

1. Crack the eggs into a large bowl and add a pinch of salt and pepper to it.
2. Use a fork to whisk the eggs until frothy and smooth
3. Melt the butter in a saucepan over high heat and pour the egg mixture over the melted butter.
4. Reduce the heat to medium and let the omelet cook.
5. Once it gets firm with a little raw egg in the middle, sprinkle the mushroom, onion and cheese over it.
6. Let it cool completely until the cheese melts and the egg sets.
7. Flip the omelet and cook for a minute and transfer to a plate.
8. Serve hot and enjoy!

Nutrition Information per Serving:

Calories 510 Kcal (Fat: 43 g | Protein: 25 g | Net carb: 4 g)

Cheese-crusted omelet

Servings: 1

Course: Lunch

Ingredients

For the omelet

- 2 eggs
- 3 ounces mature cheese (shredded or sliced)
- 2 tablespoons heavy whipping cream
- Salt and ground black pepper, to taste
- 1 tablespoon coconut oil

For the filling

- 1/2 ounce baby spinach
- 2 sliced mushrooms
- 2 tablespoons cream cheese
- 2 sliced cherry tomatoes
- 1 teaspoon dried oregano

Method
1. Crack the eggs into a large bowl and add the heavy whipping cream to it.
2. Sprinkle with salt and pepper and then thoroughly whisk the contents together until smooth and frothy
3. Heat the coconut oil in a nonstick skillet over medium heat and spread the sliced or shredded cheese in the pan evenly.
4. The cheese should cover the pan completely.
5. Let it fry until it gets bubbly.
6. Now pour the whisked egg mixture carefully over the fried cheese and reduce the heat to low.
7. Allow it to cook for 4 minutes without stirring the contents.

8. Now fill one half with spinach, mushrooms, cream cheese, cherry tomatoes and dried oregano. Let it fry for 2 to 3 minutes.
9. When the egg is about to set i.e. it will be loose on the top but not too loose, turn the empty half over the topping side and close it.
10. It will form a crescent shape. Let it fry for 4 more minutes and then transfer to a plate.
11. Serve warm and enjoy the cheesy flavor!

Nutrition Information per Serving:

Calories 789 Kcal (Fat: 66 g | Protein: 41 g | Net carb: 8 g)

Keto smoked mussels' plate

Servings: 2

Course: Dinner

Ingredients

- 8 ounces smoked canned mussels (drained)
- 4 eggs
- 1 1/2 ounces baby spinach
- 2 avocados (peeled, deseeded and finely chopped)
- 2 tablespoons olive oil
- 1/2 cup mayonnaise
- Salt and pepper, to taste

Method

1. Boil the eggs and remove the shells. You can either hard boil or soft boil them.
2. Chop the boiled eggs into small bite-sized pieces and spread them in a large plate.
3. Add the mussels, baby spinach and avocado to the egg slices.
4. Sprinkle with salt and pepper and add the mayonnaise to it.
5. Mix everything together once and drizzle the olive oil over it.
6. Serve immediately and enjoy!

Nutrition Information per Serving:

Calories 1055 Kcal (Fat: 96 g | Protein: 34 g | Net carb: 7 g)

Keto cheese omelet

Servings: 2

Course: Lunch or Dinner

Ingredients

- 4 eggs
- 1/2 cup shredded cheddar cheese
- 2 tablespoons butter
- Salt and black pepper, to taste

Method

1. Crack the eggs into a mixing bowl and whisk thoroughly until smooth. It is fine if it is slightly frothy.
2. Add half of the shredded cheddar into the whisked eggs and blend them together.
3. Season with salt and pepper and mix the contents well
4. Heat a tablespoon of butter over medium-high heat in a frying pan.
5. When the pan is hot and the butter is melted, pour half of the egg mixture into the frying pan.
6. Let it cook for 2 minutes until the egg sets.
7. Now reduce the heat to low and sprinkle a tablespoon of cheddar cheese over the omelet. (You can be generous in the cheese usage)
8. Fold the omelet and transfer to a plate
9. Repeat step 5 to 7 with the remaining egg mixture.
10. Serve hot and enjoy!

Nutrition Information per Serving:

Calories 897 Kcal (Fat: 80 g | Protein: 40 g | Net carb: 4 g)

Oven Roasted Caprese Salad

Servings: 4

Type: Dinner

Ingredients:

- 10 pieces mozzarella balls (pearl size)
- 4 cups baby spinach
- 2 cups cherry tomatoes (halved)
- 4 peeled garlic cloves
- 1/4 cup fresh basil (torn)
- 2 tablespoons avocado oil
- 1 tablespoon pesto

Method:

1. Preheat oven to 400 degrees Fahrenheit
2. Line the baking tray with a foil and spread out the cherry tomatoes and garlic evenly
3. Drizzle the avocado oil over the tomatoes and mix until it is coated well
4. Bake for 30 minutes until tops brown and juices get released
5. Meanwhile, drain the liquid from mozzarella and keep it aside. Reserve one tablespoon of the drained liquid (brine) from the cheese
6. Mix the pesto with this brine and set aside
7. Remove the tomatoes from the oven and let it cool
8. Place the spinach in a large bowl and top it with the roasted garlic and tomatoes.
9. Add the pesto sauce (pesto + brine) and mozzarella balls to the bowl. Mix well.
10. Garnish with the basil leaves and serve immediately.
11. Enjoy!

Nutrition Information per Serving:

Calories 190.7 Kcal (Fat: 13.49 g | Protein: 7.79 g | Net carb: 4.58 g)

Warm Asian Broccoli Salad

Servings: 8

Type: Dinner

Ingredients:

- 12 ounces broccoli slaw (1 bag)
- 1/2 cup coconut yogurt (full-fat)
- 2 tablespoons coconut oil
- 1/2 tablespoon sesame seeds
- 1 tablespoon coconut aminos
- 1/4 teaspoon pepper
- 1 teaspoon grated fresh ginger
- 1/2 teaspoon salt
- Handful of finely chopped cilantro, for garnishing

Method:

1. Heat the coconut oil over medium-high heat in a large skillet
2. Place the broccoli slaw on the hot oil and cover the skillet.
3. Allow it to cook for 7 minutes
4. Remove the lid and stir the cooked broccoli slaw
5. Add salt, ginger, pepper and coconut aminos to the broccoli in the skillet
6. Mix well and let it cook for a minute.
7. Remove from heat and add the yogurt and sesame seeds.
8. Mix thoroughly until the flavors blend well.
9. Garnish with the cilantro and transfer to a plate
10. Serve immediately and enjoy!

Nutrition Information per Serving:
Calories 62 Kcal (Fat: 4.28 g | Protein: 1.8 g | Net carb: 3.6 g)

Keto Brownie Breakfast Muffins

Servings: 6 muffins

Type: Breakfast

Ingredients:

- 1 large egg
- 1/4 cup caramel syrup (sugar-free)
- 1/4 cup cocoa powder
- 1 teaspoon apple cider vinegar
- 1 cup flaxseed meal
- 1/2 cup pumpkin puree
- 1 tablespoon cinnamon
- 2 tablespoons coconut oil
- 1/2 tablespoon baking powder
- 1/4 cup almonds (slivered)
- 1/2 teaspoon salt
- 1 teaspoon vanilla extract

Method:

1. Preheat oven to 350 degrees Fahrenheit
2. In a large bowl, mix together salt, cocoa powder, cinnamon and baking powder until well combined. Set aside
3. Crack the egg in a separate bowl and add the caramel syrup to it.
4. Now, add the apple cider vinegar, flaxseed meal, pumpkin puree, coconut oil and vanilla to the cracked egg and caramel.
5. Mix thoroughly until the contents are blended thoroughly.
6. Pour this egg mixture into the bowl of cocoa mixture. Mix the contents until they are well-incorporated (no lumps)
7. Line a muffin tin with paper liners and pour around 1/4 cup batter into each muffin liner

8. Sprinkle the almonds over the top of each muffin and press gently using the back of the spoon.
9. Bake for 15 minutes until they set and the muffins rise.
10. Transfer to a plate and serve warm. Enjoy!

Nutrition Information per Serving:

Calories 193 Kcal (Fat: 14.09 g | Protein: 6.98 g | Net carb: 4.37 g)

Keto salad

Servings: 2

Course: Lunch or Dinner

Ingredients

- 2 eggs
- 1/2 red onion (finely chopped)
- 3 ounces turnip (washed and peeled)
- 2 ounces cherry tomatoes (halved)
- 7 ounces green beans (fresh), washed and trimmed
- 7 ounces Romaine lettuce
- 2 ounces olives
- 2 garlic cloves (finely chopped)
- 2 tablespoons olive oil
- Salt and pepper, to taste

For the dressing

- 2 tablespoons small capers
- 1/2 cup olive oil
- 1/2 tablespoon Dijon mustard
- 1 minced garlic clove
- 1 tablespoon fresh parsley
- 1/4 cup mayonnaise
- Juice of 1/2 lemon

Method

1. Place the capers in a high-speed blender and add the Dijon mustard, mayonnaise, parsley and garlic clove to it
2. Blend on high for 60 seconds until smooth.

3. Pour the olive oil and lemon juice to the blended mixture and blend again for 30 seconds until creamy and smooth
4. Transfer the dressing to a bowl and set aside
5. Boil the eggs, peel the shell and cut them into wedges. You can either hard boil or soft boil the eggs
6. Cut the peeled turnips into half-inch pieces and parboil them in lightly salted water for 5 minutes in a small pan
7. Parboil the trimmed green beans in lightly salted water for 5 minutes in another pan.
8. Rinse the boiled beans and turnip in cold water and set aside.
9. Heat the oil in a frying pan over medium-high heat and fry the green beans in it.
10. Add garlic, pepper and salt to the beans in the pan. Stir-fry until cooked through
11. Place the lettuce leaves on a plate and add the tomatoes, onion, egg wedges, fried beans, boiled turnip and olives.
12. Drizzle the dressing over it and serve immediately. Enjoy!

Nutrition Information per Serving:

Calories 957 Kcal (Fat: 85 g | Protein: 34 g | Net carb: 11 g)

Chapter Twelve: Quick Keto Meal Recipes

Keto chicken and green beans plate

Servings: 2

Course: Dinner

Ingredients

- 1 pound rotisserie chicken
- 2 tablespoons + 3 ounces butter
- 7 ounces green beans (fresh)
- Salt and pepper, to taste

Method

1. Melt 2 tablespoons of butter over medium heat in a skillet and fry the green beans for 2 to 3 minutes
2. Season it with salt and butter and mix thoroughly.
3. Transfer the fried beans to a serving plate and add the rotisserie chicken to it.
4. Top it generously with the remaining butter and serve warm. Enjoy!

Nutrition Information per Serving:

Calories 1009 Kcal (Fat: 89 g | Protein: 48 g | Net carb: 5 g)

Keto fried halloumi cheese with mushrooms

Servings: 2

Course: Lunch

Ingredients

- 10 ounces halloumi cheese
- 10 ounces mushrooms (rinsed and trimmed)
- 10 green olives (halved)
- 3 ounces butter
- 1/2 cup mayonnaise
- Salt and pepper, to taste

Method

1. Heat 2 tablespoons of butter over medium heat in a large skillet.
2. Add the trimmed mushroom to the hot butter and fry it for 5 minutes until they become golden brown.
3. Season it with pepper and salt. Mix until combined well.
4. Add the halloumi cheese to the skillet and fry for 3 more minutes. You can add more butter if required.
5. Continue to stir the contents frequently to avoid the contents getting burn.
6. Reduce the heat and add the remaining butter. Give the contents a nice stir.
7. Transfer the fried cheesy mushrooms into a plate and serve with the olives.
8. Enjoy!

Nutrition Information per Serving:

Calories 830 Kcal (Fat: 74 g | Protein: 36 g | Net carb: 7 g)

Keto egg butter with smoked salmon and avocado

Servings: 2

Course: Lunch

Ingredients

- 4 eggs
- 4 ounces smoked salmon
- 5 ounces butter
- 2 avocados (chopped)
- 1 tablespoon chopped parsley (fresh)
- 2 tablespoons olive oil
- 1/2 teaspoon sea salt
- 1/4 teaspoon ground black pepper

Method

1. Fill a pot with cold water and place the eggs carefully in it. Place the pot on the stop top and bring the water to boil over high heat. Do not cover the pot.
2. Reduce the heat to low and allow it to simmer for 8 minutes.
3. Fill a bowl with ice-cold water and keep ready
4. Remove the eggs from hot water and immerse them in the ice-cold water.
5. Let it cool and peel the shells off the egg.
6. Chop the eggs into bite-sized pieces and place them in a large bowl.
7. Add the butter to the egg pieces and season it with salt and pepper.
8. Mix well until the flavors blend well. Garnish with parsley and transfer to a plate.
9. You can either crumble the smoked salmon with a fork and mix it with the butter-egg mixture or serve it separately along with the butter-egg mixture.

10. Add the diced avocado to the egg-salmon mixture and drizzle the olive oil over it.
11. Serve immediately and enjoy!

Nutrition Information per Serving:

Calories 1278 Kcal (Fat: 116 g | Protein: 50 g | Net carb: 5 g)

Keto fried chicken with broccoli

Servings: 2

Course: Dinner

Ingredients

- 10 ounces chicken thighs (boneless)
- 9 ounces broccoli (rinsed and trimmed)
- 1/2 cup mayonnaise
- 3 1/2 ounces butter
- Salt and pepper, to taste

Method

1. Cut the trimmed broccoli along with its stem into small bite-sized pieces and set aside
2. Heat 3 tablespoons of butter (or a generous dollop) over medium heat in a large nonstick skillet.
3. Season the chicken pieces with salt and pepper. Place this chicken on the hot butter in the skillet and fry for 5 minutes.
4. Flip the side and continue to fry until it is completely cooked through and turns golden brown.
5. Once done, add more butter (2 or 3 tablespoons) to the skillet.
6. Add the chopped broccoli to the skillet and fry for 2 to 3 minutes until the broccoli turns crisp and is completely cooked.
7. If required, season with more pepper and transfer to a plate.
8. Serve hot with the remaining butter and enjoy!

Nutrition Information per Serving:

Calories 733Kcal (Fat: 66 g | Protein: 29 g | Net carb: 5 g)

Keto lamb chops with herb butter

Servings: 4

Course: Lunch

Ingredients

- 8 lamb chops
- 4 ounces herb butter
- 1 tablespoon butter
- 1 lemon (cut into wedges)
- 1 tablespoon olive oil
- Salt and pepper, to taste

Method

1. If the lamb chops are too cold, let it sit until it reaches the room temperature before you begin cooking.
2. Once the lamb chops are ready, season them with salt and pepper.
3. Brush the olive oil over the lamb chops and grill them until you get the brown surface
4. Or you can also fry the lamb chops in butter over medium heat for 5 minutes until completely cooked through and golden brown.
5. Transfer the fried chops to a plate and top it with herb butter. Garnish with lemon wedges and serve warm. Enjoy

Nutrition Information per Serving:

Calories 729 Kcal (Fat: 62 g | Protein: 43 g | Net carb: 0.3 g)

Keto Tex-Mex burger plate

Servings: 2

Course: Dinner

Ingredients

- 10 ounces ground beef
- 1 tablespoon Tex-Mex seasoning
- 2 avocados (peeled, deseeded and mashed)
- 1/2 cup mayonnaise
- 4 ounces sliced Mexican cheese
- 2 ounces arugula lettuce
- 2 tablespoons pickled jalapeños
- 2 tablespoons cold water
- Salt and pepper, to taste
- 2 tablespoons olive oil

Method

1. Place the ground beef in a large bowl and add 2 tablespoons cold water to it.
2. Add the Tex-Mex seasoning to the beef and mix well until the contents are incorporated.
3. Make a burger from the mixture and brush it with olive oil on all sides.
4. Grill for 4 minutes on both sides until it gets cooked well. Flip to the other side and grill for another 3 minutes.
5. Season with salt and pepper as per your taste.
6. Repeat step 3 to step 5 with the remaining mixture and transfer the burgers to a plate.
7. Take a serving plate and place one burger on it. Add the mashed avocado, jalapenos and the cheese. Spread a generous amount of mayonnaise and place a lettuce on it.

8. Cover it with another burger and drizzle a bit of olive oil.
9. Serve warm and enjoy!

Nutrition Information per Serving:

Calories 951 Kcal (Fat: 82 g | Protein: 39 g | Net carb: 7 g)

Keto Caprese omelet

Servings: 2

Course: Lunch or Dinner

Ingredients

- 6 eggs
- 5 ounces mozzarella cheese (fresh)
- 3 ounces cherry tomatoes cut in halves
- 2 tablespoons olive oil
- 1 tablespoon basil (fresh or dried)
- Salt and pepper, to taste

Method

1. Take a mixing bowl and crack the eggs into it. Add salt and pepper to the cracked eggs.
2. Whisk together using a form until well combined.
3. Add the basil to the whisked egg and mix well.
4. Slice the cheese and keep aside.
5. Heat the olive oil in a large pan over medium heat.
6. Add the cherry tomatoes to the hot oil and fry for 3 minutes until cooked through
7. Pour the egg mixture over the tomatoes and let it cook for a while.
8. When the egg is slightly firm, add the cheese slices over the top.
9. Reduce the heat and let the omelet cook until it is completely set.
10. Transfer to a plate and serve hot. Enjoy!

Nutrition Information per Serving:

Calories 534 Kcal (Fat: 43 g | Protein: 33 g | Net carb: 4 g)

Keto ground beef and green beans

Servings: 2

Course: Dinner

Ingredients

- 9 ounces green beans (fresh), rinsed and trimmed
- 10 ounces ground beef
- 1/2 cup mayonnaise
- 3 1/2 ounces butter
- Salt and pepper, to taste

Method

1. Heat 2 tablespoons of butter in a large pan over medium heat.
2. Add the ground beef to the hot butter and cook on high heat until the beef is completely browned.
3. Season the mixture with salt and pepper.
4. Reduce the heat to low and add some more butter.
5. Add the trimmed beans and fry for another 5 minutes until it is cooked through.
6. Stir frequently and let the contents cook for some time. Add more salt and pepper if you prefer.
7. Transfer the fried beef and beans to a plate and serve with mayonnaise.
8. Enjoy!

Nutrition Information per Serving:

Calories 694 Kcal (Fat: 60 g | Protein: 32 g | Net carb: 5 g)

Keto chicken salad

Servings: 4

Course: Lunch

Ingredients

- 1 pound chicken thighs (boneless)
- 10 ounces Romaine lettuce (rinse and drain)
- 4 ounces cherry tomatoes (halved)
- 1 ounces butter
- 1/2 tablespoons garlic powder
- 3/4 cup mayonnaise
- Salt and pepper, to taste

Method

1. Prepare the garlic mayonnaise by mixing the mayonnaise and garlic powder in a small bowl. Set the prepared mixture aside.
2. Shred the chicken and place it in another bowl. Season it with salt and pepper. Toss it over to get the flavor blended.
3. Heat the butter in a large pan over medium heat.
4. Add the chicken to the hot butter and stir-fry until thoroughly cooked and golden brown
5. Take a clean cutting board and shred the lettuce using a sharp knife.
6. Transfer the shredded lettuce into a plate and top it with fried chicken, cherry tomatoes and garlic mayonnaise
7. Serve warm and enjoy!

Nutrition Information per Serving:

Calories 394 Kcal (Fat: 33 g | Protein: 21 g | Net carb: 2 g)

Chapter Thirteen: Keto Snack and Dessert Recipes

Keto Flan

Servings: 4

Course: Dessert

Ingredients

- 2 eggs (large ones)
- 1 cup heavy whipping cream
- 2 egg yolks (of large eggs)
- 1 tablespoon butter
- 1/8 cup water
- 1 tablespoon vanilla
- 1/3 cup erythritol, for caramel + 1/4 cup erythritol for custard

Method

1. Heat the 1/3-cup erythritol in a deep pan over medium heat. Keep stirring more than often.
2. Add the water and butter to the erythritol and continue stirring until you get the golden-brown texture of the caramel
3. Take 4 ramekins and pour this caramel equally covering the ramekin's bottom perfectly.
4. Set it aside and allow them to cool
5. Take another bowl and transfer the remaining 1/4-cup erythritol into it.
6. Add the vanilla and heavy whipping cream and mix thoroughly until well-combined
7. Crack the eggs in another bowl and whisk them using a fork. Slowly add the egg yolks and whisk the contents together until smooth
8. Add this egg mixture to the erythritol-cream mixture as you slowly stir the contents.
9. Pour this mixture (custard) over the top of the set caramel in each ramekin.

10. Fill half of a casserole dish with hot water and place the ramekins carefully in this hot water such that they float
11. Bake this at 350 degrees Fahrenheit by placing the casserole dish into the oven.
12. Take out the casserole dish from the oven after the baking time but don't remove the ramekins from the hot water.
13. Let it stand for another 10 minutes
14. Take out the ramekins using a tong and refrigerate overnight or for minimum 4 hours
15. When you are ready to serve, run the inside of the custard with a knife to slowly release it from the ramekin.
16. Turn it upside down onto a plate and jiggle the custard out.
17. Serve chilled and enjoy!

Nutrition Information per Serving:

Calories 297 Kcal (Fat: 31.5 g | Protein: 4.5 g | Net carb: 2.4 g)

Keto Butter Pecan Ice cream (Low Carb)

Servings: 8 (1/2 cup each)

Course: Dessert

Ingredients

- 1/4 cup butter
- 2 tablespoons pecans (toasted and chopped)
- 1 tablespoon MCT oil
- 2 cups heavy cream
- 2 egg yolks
- 1 tablespoon Choczero Maple Pecan sweetener
- 1/4 teaspoon salt
- 1/2 cup Swerve sweetener confectioner
- 2 teaspoon maple extract

Method

1. Heat a small saucepan over low heat and melt the butter in it.
2. Add the swerve sweetener, salt and heavy cream to the melted butter. Stir occasionally until heated through. Do not boil! Set this mixture aside
3. Whisk the egg yolks in another bowl until it becomes light in color.
4. Add a spoon of the prepared butter-cream mixture to the whisked egg.
5. Stir it well to temper them and continue adding two or more spoons as you stir the mixture.
6. Now add the yolk mixture back to the buttercream mixture on the stove.
7. Keep stirring as the mixture continues to thicken over low heat. The thickness of the mixture should be such that if you

spoon it, then it should form a layer of coating in the back of the spoon.
8. Pour this mixture into a small bowl and refrigerate for 30 minutes.
9. After 30 minutes, add the MCT oil, maple extract and maple pecan sweetener to the bowl.
10. Mix thoroughly until well combined and now pour this creamy mixture in the ice cream machine.
11. Follow the manufacturer's instructions and then slowly add the pecans into it.
12. Once ready, transfer the ice cream into a loaf pan (8 X 5) and freeze for 3 hours
13. Serve the soft ice cream in a bowl and enjoy!

Nutrition Information per Serving:

Calories 302 Kcal (Fat: 32 g | Protein: 2 g | Net carb: 1 g)

Keto Vanilla Pound cake

Servings: 3 to 4

Course: Dessert

Ingredients

- 4 large eggs
- 1 teaspoon vanilla extract
- 2 cups almond flour
- 2 teaspoons baking powder
- 1/2 cup butter
- 1 cup sour cream
- 1 cup Erythritol
- 2 ounces cream cheese

Method

1. Preheat the oven to 350 degrees Fahrenheit.
2. Grease a 9-inch Bundt pan generously with butter and set aside.
3. Place the almond flour in a large bowl and add the baking powder into it. Mix to combine and set aside
4. Slice the remaining butter into small squares (as many as you can) and place them in a separate bowl.
5. Add the cream cheese into the butter bowl and microwave this for 30 seconds (do not burn the cheese).
6. Remove from the microwave and let it cool for some time.
7. Mix the cheese and butter well until combined.
8. Now add the sour cream, erythritol and vanilla extract to the cheese-butter mixture and mix well.
9. Pour this mixture into the almond-baking powder mixture and stir well until the contents are incorporated.

10. Crack the eggs into this batter and stir thoroughly until all the ingredients are well combined.
11. Pour this well-mixed batter into the greased Bundt pan and bake for 50 minutes in the oven
12. Insert a toothpick through the cake and check if it comes out clean.
13. Remove from the oven and let it cool in room temperature for some time.
14. Refrigerate overnight or for minimum two hours before you serve and relish!

Nutrition Information per Serving:

Calories 249 Kcal (Fat: 20.67 g | Protein: 7.67 g | Net carb: 5.23 g)

Churro Mug Cake

Servings: 1

Course: Dessert

Ingredients

For the base

- 1 large egg
- 1/2 teaspoon baking powder
- 1 tablespoon erythritol
- 2 tablespoons almond flour
- 2 tablespoons butter
- 7 drops of liquid Stevia

For the flavor

- 2 tablespoons almond flour
- 1/8 teaspoon allspice powder
- 1/4 teaspoon ground cinnamon
- 1/4 teaspoon vanilla
- 1/4 teaspoon ground nutmeg
- 1/8 teaspoon ground ginger

For the topping

- 1 tablespoon heavy whipping cream
- 1 tablespoon finely chopped almonds

Method

1. Keep your mug ready – a nice big one!

2. Crack the egg into a large bowl and add 2 tablespoons of almond flour, baking powder, erythritol and liquid stevia into it
3. Mix together until the contents blend well. Slowly add the butter and mix again until you get a lump-less mixture
4. Place the remaining 2 tablespoons almond flour in another bowl and add the allspice, cinnamon, vanilla, nutmeg and ginger.
5. Mix the contents together until well combined.
6. Pour the egg-butter mixture into the mug and add the flour mixture into it.
7. Mix them together thoroughly and microwave on 10 (power level) for 60 seconds
8. Once done, turn the mug upside down over a plate and lightly tap it to get the cake out.
9. Top the cake with the heavy whipping cream and almond bits.
10. Serve immediately and enjoy!

Nutrition Information per Serving:

Calories 447 Kcal (Fat: 42.03 g | Protein: 12.61 g | Net carb: 4.77g)

Jicama Fries

Servings: 2

Course: Snack

Ingredients

- 1 jicama (peeled and sliced into thin strips)
- 1/2 teaspoon onion powder
- 2 tablespoons avocado oil
- Cayenne pepper (pinch)
- 1 teaspoon paprika
- Sea salt, to taste

Method

1. Dry roast the jicama strips in a non-stick frying pan (or you can also grease the pan with a bit of avocado oil)
2. Place the roasted jicama fries into a large bowl and add the onion powder, cayenne pepper, paprika and sea salt.
3. Drizzle over the avocado oil and toss the contents until the flavors are incorporated well.
4. Serve immediately and enjoy!

Nutrition Information per Serving:

Calories 92 Kcal (Fat: 7 g | Protein: 1 g | Net carb: 2 g)

Tropical Coconut Balls

Servings: 2

Course: Snack

Ingredients

- 1 cup shredded coconut (unsweetened)
- 6 tablespoons coconut milk (full-fat)
- 2 tablespoons melted coconut oil
- 1/4 cup almond flour
- 2 tablespoons lemon juice
- 2 tablespoons ground chia seeds
- Zest of 1 lemon
- 10 drops stevia (alcohol-free)
- 1/8 teaspoons sea salt

Method

1. Preheat the oven to 250 degrees Fahrenheit
2. Place the shredded coconut in a large bowl and pour the coconut milk into it.
3. Add the almond flour, ground chia, sea salt, coconut oil, and lemon zest and lemon juice to the bowl.
4. Mix everything together until well combined.
5. Take 1 tablespoon of the mixture and form a ball out of it. Repeat with the remaining mixture.
6. Line a baking tray with parchment paper and place the small balls on it.
7. If you find the mixture too dry while making the balls, add one tablespoon (extra) of coconut oil to the mixture
8. Bake the coconut balls for 30 minutes and remove from the oven.
9. Let it cool completely at room temperature.
10. Transfer the balls into another container carefully and refrigerate it for 30 minutes.

11. Serve chilled and enjoy!

Nutrition Information per Serving:

Calories 134 Kcal (Fat: 13.1 g | Protein: 2.2 g | Net carb: 1.1 g)

Zucchini Fries with Almond Flour

Servings: 2

Course: Snack

Ingredients

- 1 large zucchini
- 1 teaspoon black pepper
- 1/2 cup almond flour
- 1 egg
- 1 teaspoon paprika
- 4 tablespoons coconut oil

Method

1. Slice the zucchini into small sticks with a sharp knife. You don't need to peel the skin. Set this aside.
2. Place the almond flour in a plate and add the pepper and paprika to it.
3. Fold carefully to combine the dry mixture and set it aside
4. Crack the egg in a small bowl and beat it thoroughly.
5. Add all the zucchini sticks to the egg bowl and toss it well until it is completely coated with the egg
6. Now roll this egg-coated zucchini sticks in flour mixture until all the surfaces are covered with the spice-flour mix
7. Heat the coconut oil in a shallow frying pan over high heat
8. Drop the spice-coated zucchini sticks gently into the hot oil and let it fry until brown
9. Transfer the fried sticks on a plate lined with paper towel to drain the excess oil
10. Serve hot and enjoy!

Nutrition Information per Serving:

Calories 142 Kcal (Fat: 9 g | Protein: 10 g | Net carb: 4 g)

Keto Peanut Butter Cookies

Servings: 15 cookies approximately

Course: Snack

Ingredients

- 1 cup peanut butter (unsweetened)
- 2 tablespoons Erythritol
- 1 teaspoon cocoa powder
- Salt, to taste
- 1 large egg

Method

1. Preheat oven at 300 degrees Fahrenheit
2. Crack the egg in a large bowl and add the peanut butter and erythritol to it.
3. Whisk the contents together until well-combined
4. Add the cocoa powder and a pinch of salt. Mix thoroughly.
5. Line a baking tray with parchment paper and spoon out the mixture onto the tray
6. Press the mixture using the back of the spoon to form a cookie shape.
7. Bake for 15 minutes until heated through and browned
8. Serve warm and enjoy!

Nutrition Information per Serving:

Calories 70 Kcal (Fat: 6 g | Protein: 3 g | Net carb: 1 g)

Eggplant Chips with Herbs and Olive Oil

Servings: 3

Course: Snack

Ingredients

- 1 medium eggplant (unpeeled)
- 1/4 teaspoon black pepper
- 1/4 teaspoon cayenne pepper
- 1/2 teaspoon paprika
- 1/4 teaspoon dried dill
- 1/4 teaspoon oregano
- 1 tablespoon olive oil
- Salt, to taste

Method

1. Slice the eggplant into thin strips and spread them out in a large plate
2. Season it with salt and let it sit for one hour.
3. If you find the water draining from the sliced eggplant, discard it regularly
4. Preheat the oven to 350 degrees Fahrenheit
5. Mix together the cayenne pepper, dried dill, oregano, paprika and black pepper in a small bowl.
6. Season the eggplant slices with this spice mixture on both the sides.
7. Drizzle over the olive oil on the spice-coated eggplant on both the sides.
8. Spread them in the baking tray and bake for 30 minutes until crispy
9. Serve warm and enjoy!

Nutrition Information per Serving:

Calories 86 Kcal (Fat: 4.94 g | Protein: 1.94 g | Net carb: 4.44 g)

Keto Parmesan Crisps with Tomato Slices

Servings: 3

Course: Snack

Ingredients

- 1/2 tomato thinly sliced (small one)
- 1/2 cup freshly grated parmesan cheese
- 1/8 teaspoon black pepper
- 1/8 teaspoon chili powder

Method

1. Preheat the oven to 390 degrees Fahrenheit
2. Place the grated Parmesan in a bowl and add the chili powder and black pepper to it.
3. Mix well and spread the spice-mixed Parmesan on a baking tray.
4. Bake them for 5 minutes until crispy and add the sliced tomatoes over them.
5. Bake for 2 more minutes and remove from the oven.
6. Let it cool for 5 minutes and transfer to a plate.
7. Serve immediately and enjoy!

Nutrition Information per Serving:

Calories 147 Kcal (Fat: 9.58 g | Protein: 12.97 g | Net carb: 1.84 g)

Mini Low Carb Cheesecakes with Blackberry

Servings: 4

Course: Dessert

Ingredients

- 4 eggs
- 1/4 cup blackberry
- 2 ounces cream cheese
- 2 tablespoons stevia
- 1/2 cup butter (unsalted)
- 1/4 cup water
- 1/8 teaspoon baking powder

Method

1. Preheat the oven to 450 degrees Fahrenheit
2. Blend the cream cheese, 1/2 tablespoon stevia and butter in a high-speed blender for 45 seconds until creamy and smooth
3. Crack the eggs into the blender and add the baking powder to the cheese butter mix.
4. Blend again for another 60 seconds on high until creamy and thick
5. Place the remaining stevia into a small skillet and pour the water into it.
6. Heat this on low heat as you continue to stir. Take half of the berries and crush them gently.
7. Add these crushed berries into the stevia water and let it cook for 10 minutes.
8. Soon enough you will get a jelly-like mixture forming in the skillet.
9. Grease a cupcake cup with a bit of butter and pour this jelly mixture into the cup

10. Transfer the cheese cream mixture over the jelly mixture and keep it ready
11. Take a baking tray and pour some water into it. Arrange the cupcake cup over the water in the tray
12. Bake for 35 minutes until the cake is thoroughly baked
13. Insert a toothpick and see if it comes out clean.
14. Remove from the oven and let it cool.
15. Refrigerate it for 2 hours before you serve. Enjoy!

Nutrition Information per Serving:

Calories 347 Kcal (Fat: 34.7 g | Protein: 8.1 g | Net carb: 1.6 g)

Peanut Butter Caramel Milkshake

Servings: 1

Course: Dessert

Ingredients

- 2 tablespoons peanut butter
- 1 cup unsweetened coconut milk (full-fat)
- 2 tablespoons salted caramel (sugar-free)
- 1 tablespoon MCT oil

Methods

1. Pour the coconut milk into a high-speed blender and add a tablespoon of MCT oil to it.
2. Now, add the salted caramel and peanut butter into the blender.
3. Blend on high for 60 seconds until smooth and creamy
4. If you want it to be served chilled, you can add few ice cubes and blend once more for 45 seconds until the smooth and thick.
5. Transfer to a glass and serve chilled. Enjoy!

Nutrition Information per Serving:

Calories 369 Kcal (Fat: 34.95 g | Protein: 8.1 g | Net carb: 7.53 g)

Conclusion

We have come to the end of this book. We would like to take this opportunity to thank you once again for choosing this book.

The book has covered the primary objective, which is to serve as a complete guide for readers to learn about the ketogenic diet and its various health benefits. The chapters concentrate on giving a brief description on ketosis, the details on how to get started with a keto diet, a complete keto meal plan and a quick shopping list. The chapters also focus on the list of foods that can (or cannot) be consumed and the effect this lifestyle has on an individual's health.

The book has simple and easy to cook recipes for you to have a complete keto diet plan.

We sincerely hope this book was useful and has helped to answer most of the queries you had in mind.

Thank you and best wishes!

Amy Crenn & Suzanne Rodriguez

Sources

https://hvmn.com/library/ketosis/keto-diet-fundamentals

https://www.womenshealthmag.com/weight-loss/a19434332/what-is-the-keto-diet/

https://www.nerdfitness.com/blog/the-beginners-guide-to-the-keto-diet-or-ketogenic-diet/

https://hvmn.com/library/ketosis/keto-diet-fundamentals

https://www.healthline.com/nutrition/ketogenic-diet-101#faq

https://www.dietdoctor.com/low-carb/keto/foods

https://www.healthline.com/health/food-nutrition/keto-shopping-list#download-the-guide

https://theketoqueens.com/sweeteners-you-can-use-on-a-keto-diet/

https://theketoqueens.com/low-carb-vegetables-keto-vegetable-food-lists/

https://theketoqueens.com/beginner-keto-grocery-list/

https://www.aaaai.org/conditions-and-treatments/conditions-dictionary/food-intolerance

http://ketosister.com/keto-problems-food-allergies-sensitivities/

https://missfitliving.com/keto-mistakes/

https://www.dietdoctor.com/low-carb/keto/common-questions#isaketodietsafe

https://www.dietdoctor.com/low-carb/keto/common-questions#howdoyouknowhenyourbodyisinketosis

https://www.dietdoctor.com/low-carb/keto/common-questions#isaketodietsafeforthekidneys

https://medium.com/@timferriss/how-to-lose-20-pounds-of-fat-in-30-days-without-doing-any-exercise-551b00ccb352

https://www.ruled.me/30-day-ketogenic-diet-plan/

https://www.ruled.me/ketogenic-diet-shopping-list/

Enjoy this book? You can make a big difference

Reviews are the most powerful tools in our arsenal when it comes getting attention for our books. Much as we'd like to, we don't have the financial muscle of a New York publisher. We can't take out full page ads in the newspaper or put posters on the subway.

(Not yet, anyway)

But we do have something much more powerful and effective than that, and it's something that those publishers would kill to get their hands on.

A committed and loyal bunch of readers.

Honest reviews of our books help bring them to the attention of other readers.

If you've enjoyed this book We would be very grateful if you could spend just five minutes leaving a review (it can be as short as you like) on the book's Amazon page.

Thank you very much.

Made in the USA
Columbia, SC
14 July 2019